PHILIP GREENSLADE
GOD'S
QUESTIONS

PHILIP GREENSLADE

GOD'S
QUESTIONS

Responding to the first five questions
God asks every one of us

Copyright © CWR 2003

Published 2003 by CWR, Waverley Abbey House, Waverley Lane, Farnham,
Surrey GU9 8EP.

The right of Philip Greenslade to be identified as the author of this work
has been asserted in accordance with the Copyright, Designs and Patents
Act 1988, sections 77 and 78.

All rights reserved. No part of this publication may be reproduced, stored in
a retrieval system, or transmitted, in any form or by any means, electronic,
mechanical, photocopying, recording or otherwise, without the prior
permission in writing of CWR.

See back of book for list of National Distributors.

Unless otherwise indicated, all Scripture references are from the Holy Bible:
New International Version (NIV), copyright © 1973, 1978, 1984 by the
International Bible Society.

Concept development, editing, design and production by CWR.

Printed in England by Cox & Wyman.

ISBN 1-85345-259-9

CONTENTS

PREFACE

This small book sets itself to consider the first five questions God asks the human race after the Fall. Its starting point is Abraham Heschel's judgment that

> the Bible maintains that the question about God is a question of God. If the Lord did not ask the question, in vain would be the labour of those who deal with it. God is in search of man and life is something that requires an answer.[1]

'Where are you?' (Gen. 3:9) raises the *theological* question of our lost (and restored) relationship with God. It explores issues of shame and alienation, and the mechanisms we adopt to hide from the reality of God; it raises hopes of homecoming and reconciliation. The question introduces us to a God who loves us enough to ask the tough questions and comes looking for us with the tender love and searching grace revealed in Jesus.

'Who told you?' (Gen. 3:11) raises the *ideological* question of where we get our ideas from. This question seeks to alert us to the cultural indoctrination and parental programming we have been subject to. It explores the issue of truth in a postmodern world and introduces us to the God who speaks truth in Scripture, who incarnates truth in Jesus, and

whose voice alone we can trust to lead us into reliable reality.

'What is this you have done?' (Gen. 3:13) raises the *moral* question of how far we are responsible for our words and deeds. It explores the nature of guilt and the boundaries of moral responsibility. This question explores themes such as scapegoating, forgiveness and atonement and how good works flow from grace and redemption.

'Why are you angry?' (Gen. 4:6) raises the *psychological* question of the sources of our emotions and what our feelings tell us about our self-esteem or self-hatred, our jealousy and anger. It introduces us to the God whose gospel is the path to healing and wholeness for the whole person.

'Where is your brother?' (Gen. 4:9) raises the *social* question of how our individuality defined in the image of God is set in a social context. The question explores violations of that image as what distorts, damages or destroys the image of God that is our original stamp of grandeur and dignity. It introduces us to the redemption and grace that recreates the community of the one new humanity in Christ.

So much for the *content* of the book. A word about its *style*. Each chapter follows a roughly similar pattern:

- the Genesis narrative
- Old Testament connections
- the parable of the Prodigal Son
- the cross, noting particularly the words Jesus speaks from the cross.

As for the tone of the book, I hope you will detect a number of concerns. I write, first, with *a sense of urgency about asking the right questions*. This book represents a determination not to settle for premature answers or quick-fix solutions. I recall an old cartoon, which showed a man holding up a billboard saying, 'Jesus is the answer'; alongside him another person was holding a placard which reads, 'What is the question?' As Earl Palmer says,

> We make the best discoveries when we cease trying to ensure that the answers of Jesus always support the prearranged solutions that we so badly want, or think we want. I make the best discoveries when I quit trying to force every theme of the Bible to answer the questions I decide are the most important questions.[2]

This book is written in the spirit of Frederick Buechner's advice: 'Don't start looking at the Bible for the answers it gives. Start by listening to the questions it asks.'[3] I share with you, then, my conviction that the truly important questions are not those we ask God but the questions He asks us!

Second, as I write, I am only too *well aware of just how complex life is*. Good news does not come as easy answers, and is not told well in the conventional clichés of 'greetings-card-Christianity'. God moves in mysterious ways His saving wonders to perform. As Psalm 139 reminds us, we also are a mystery, at least to ourselves. As for sin, it too is irrational, the very 'mystery of iniquity'. Simplistic slogans will not breach the walls of unbelief nor will cheap grace keep us free. So something of the spirit of Kierkegaard haunts these pages. He confessed that for love of mankind, despair at his own embarrassment, and moved by genuine interest in those who made everything easy, he had conceived it as his task 'to create difficulties everywhere'![4]

I would like, third, to *entice you into an encounter with the wildness of God*. God is good but He is not safe. Responding to God's questions is not a recipe for eliminating danger or avoiding risk. The confidence we have as Christians does not rest on our own logical prowess, but derives from God's self-revelation in Scripture and Spirit. We are graciously offered a share in the certain assurance with which God knows Himself. So I write in the spirit of Daniel Taylor when he says,

> While certainty is beyond our reach, meaning – something far more valuable – is not. Meaning derives from our right relationship with God, based not on certainty and conformity, but on risk and commitment.[5]

PREFACE

Take W.H. Auden's advice: 'He is the way; follow him through the land of unlikeness; you will see rare beasts and have unique adventures.'

Lastly, these reflections are offered by *someone who relies upon and relishes God's grace*. There is much about such grace in this book. But in my experience this is tough grace. Grace is not the spiritual equivalent of stroking. It rescues us for heaven, but reclaims us also for earth. As practised by a God of holy love, grace both approves us and commands us. Grace undoubtedly inspires us; it also instructs us.

> For the grace of God that brings salvation has appeared to all men. It teaches us to say 'No' to ungodliness and worldly passions, and to live self-controlled, upright and godly lives in this present age, while we wait for the blessed hope – the glorious appearing of our great God and Saviour, Jesus Christ, who gave himself for us to redeem us from all wickedness and to purify for himself a people that are his very own, eager to do what is good.
>
> Titus 2:11–14

'No ... self-control ... wait' – what three words could be more countercultural than these? Yet grace makes us hopeful, free and passionate about doing good to people. So I write in the spirit of Lewis Smedes:

> Grace is too unpredictable, too lavish, too delicious for

us to stay sober about it. What can you do with such unchecked generosity but smack your lips, slosh it around your tongue, and savor it with joy?[6]

I need to thank the usual cast of suspects. Quotations are liberally scattered throughout. Who was it who said that 'the best writers seldom quote from other authors' and that 'footnotes are the confetti at a marriage of small minds'? (Oh well, I made that up, but you get my drift.) I am not above calling on a 'great cloud of witnesses' for two reasons: to indicate the kind of books you might consider reading, and to acknowledge those who have helped to make this the kind of book I might consider reading.

My good friend Trevor Martin has once more contributed his enjoyable friendship and editorial flair to the task. I am grateful to him, and to the expertise of the design and production team at CWR.

Mary – to whom I 'popped the question' some 35 years ago – has added loving wisdom to the project and continues to forgive a husband who does not have all the answers but believes he has the ones that count.

Philip Greenslade
November 2002

INVITATION

'Finding the right questions is as crucial as finding the right answers.'

Henri Nouwen

Life, in truth, is a long-drawn-out question. Whether through joy, pain or outright boredom, the sheer fact of being alive raises many questions, not least the meaning of life itself. In a classic *Peanuts* cartoon,[1] Charlie Brown has gone to bed in reflective mood.

> Sometimes I lie awake at night and ask: 'Is life a multiple choice test or is it a true-or-false test?' Then a voice comes to me out of the dark: 'We hate to tell you this but life is a thousand-word essay!'

Until very recent times most people sensed this and pondered life's enigmatic quality. But the twentieth century's cataclysmic suffering has numbed our curiosity and left us feeling helpless. At the same time, its technological advances left us speechless while its consumer benefits preoccupied our waking hours. One perceptive thinker, P.T. Forsyth, noted over a century ago that such self-absorption in his day had not yet quite silenced the big questions:

13

There are happily still people who ask what all the long and tragic train of history means, what great things does it intend …? They ask what is it all worth at last … has history a destiny worth its aweful cost? Do all its throbbing sorrows, its soaring aspirations, its tragedies sordid or sublime, its dreadful conflicts, its splendid achievements, its miserable failures, its broken hearts and ruined civilisations … do they all draw together to a due close?

'Or,' on the other hand, as Forsyth put it to his contemporaries, 'are you so happy with the children, or so engrossed in your enterprises, that you can spare no attention to ask about the movement, the meaning, the fate of the race?'[2]

Developments since, in our postmodern world, have seemingly confirmed Forsyth's fears. In today's flip and ironic mood, we have become more accustomed to the shrug of the shoulder than the bending of the knee, more used to the raised eyebrow than the leap of joy. So the urgent cry of 'why?' from those scared witless has subsided into a dismissive 'whatever?' from the bored and self-interested. Recently only the terrible events of 11 September 2001 have threatened to disturb our self-enclosed materialistic mindset. Currently the spectre of global terrorism is concentrating the Western mind, if not wonderfully at least worryingly. Ultimate questions won't go away.

In Daniel Migliore's words, 'Human life ceases to be human not when we do not have all the answers but when we no longer have the courage to ask the really important questions.'[3] It is for this reason that I want to draw your attention to *the questions God asks*, which are the ultimate questions.

ANY QUESTIONS?

It is, of course, commonplace for even non-believers to find themselves asking God questions. 'Why doesn't He prevent evil things happening?' 'Why do the innocent suffer?' 'Why is there so much injustice?' Believers ask these things too, together with, 'When will my prayers be answered?' And many more in similar vein.

Questions like these naturally rise to the surface when life's sediment is churned up by guilt, illness, injustice, redundancy or bereavement. And genuine faith does not close down these questions as if they were inappropriate. The answers to them do not come easily but we have ample scriptural encouragement to ask them without fear of offending an over-sensitive God.[4] All this is valid and healthy. But what I am advocating in this book is that true faith spurs us to probe further and enables us to face a deeper reality by meeting the questioning God.

Asking God questions is one thing: answering God's questions is quite another. In my experience, tuning in to

15

God's questions, although usually disconcerting, is a life-changing encounter.

Henri Nouwen astutely points out that the nature of the questions we consider is as important as the answers to our questions.

> Which questions guide our lives? Which questions do we make our own? Which questions deserve our undivided attention and full personal commitment? Finding the right questions is as crucial as finding the right answers.[5]

For Christians everywhere, the Bible remains the source for finding the right questions and, as essential priorities, the crucial first five questions God asks every one of us. It is quite possible to approach the Bible with a list of the queries we deem to be important and demand that the Bible answer them. Indeed some people treat the Bible as if it were a *Yellow Pages* of theology or ethics. If they want their spiritual plumbing fixed they have only to walk the pages to get the solution! But biblical faith never provides so easy a palliative. God loves us too much to offer us a mere placebo and respects us enough not to fob us off with quick-fix solutions to our deepest needs. So instead of expecting the Bible to answer all the questions we put to it, let us for once allow the Bible to confront us with the questions God asks

Bible is a book of questions rather than a book of answers.

of us. 'Rather than having all the answers,' comments Daniel Migliore,

> believers often find that they have a new set of questions … The Bible is no easy answer book, although it is sometimes read that way. If we are ready to listen, the Bible has the power to shake us violently with its terrible questions: 'Adam, where are you?' (Gen. 3:9), 'Cain, where is your brother? (Gen. 4:9).[6]

As we shall discover, responding to these questions turns out to be both a challenge and a comfort.

THE PRESSURE OF ANXIETY

One of the reasons why this is so important has to do with the spiritual and emotional climate in which our questions arise. We may not always question God angrily or accusingly. But almost invariably we ask out of the pressure of anxiety. Think of the many anxious 'what if …?' questions we ask. What if I don't find a job? What if my child isn't healed? What if my marriage doesn't change? These are very real and painful questions, which clamour for an answer. But if we are honest, they are nearly always being read off the agenda of fear. Too often it is the external forces of power in the world, rendering us helpless, that set our agenda. Listen again to Henri Nouwen and see if you agree when he says,

> The things we think about, worry about, reflect upon, and
> spend time and energy on are in large part determined
> by a world which seduces us into accepting its fearful
> questions.[7]

But again with Nouwen we may wonder if fear-filled
questions ever lead to 'love-filled answers'.[8] Such questions
seem the most pressing but they may not be the most
fundamental. It takes courage to upgrade our questions to the
ones God is asking. As Abraham Heschel puts it: 'Religion
consists of God's question and man's answer ... Unless God
asks the question, all our inquiries are in vain.'[9] Yet, it is my
conviction that stopping to listen to God's questions is the
way to find release from our 'huge network of anxiety'. Let's
pray with Henri Nouwen: 'Lord, help me, in the midst of this
anxiety-provoking world to live in the house of love and
there to listen to the questions raised by the Lord of love.'[10]

We may well end up asking ourselves: 'Am I helping God
with his inquiries?'!

THE PRESSURE OF RELEVANCE

If it is under the pressure of anxiety that we ask painful
personal questions, then it is often under the pressure of
relevance that the Church gives its public answers. Michael
Horton's is one of an increasing number of voices raised at
the way the contemporary evangelical church too readily

reacts to the agenda set by the surrounding consumer culture. 'Today,' he says,

> we want to run immediately to the 'practical'; or the 'relevant', as if God were irrelevant. We look sus-piciously at those who want to talk about theology and eternity and we say 'You have your head in the clouds, let's talk about the real problems.' But that assumes that the real problems are temporal and, if there is any time left over, we can get around to the eternal questions. That is the essence of secularism, but it is widely embraced in our own churches.[11]

This is not to argue that church studies are irrelevant and occupy a nostalgic and religious parallel universe. Luther rightly admonished, 'If you preach the gospel in all aspects with the exception of the issues which deal specifically with your time, you are not preaching the gospel.' But it is to urge the Church not to mirror the surrounding society as if unbelievers are in a position to know best what questions needed answering. It is to insist that the kingdom of God changes all the questions. It is to disturb the Church's preoccupation with pragmatic solutions and penultimate question and to keep before the world's attention those questions that are of first importance and eternal consequence. This book represents my contribution to this cause.

Donald Bloesch says it well:

> The evangelical theologian does not blithely proceed to correlate the creative questions of the culture and the answer of faith. Instead we are challenged to lead people to ask the right questions that are hidden from sinful humanity until the moment of revelation.[12]

A pragmatic age is primarily interested in hands-on answers to 'how-to …? questions. Responding to this, even a church avowedly committed to the workings of God feels pressed to develop methods and techniques – what Eugene Peterson calls a 'technology of the supernatural'[13] – in order to harness miraculous divine powers, to bring them under our control and so make them consistently available to address our felt needs. Similarly the market-driven church, in its effort to be user-friendly, dissolves truth into easily assimilated sound bites and manageable methods.

But scaling down our questions to what is being asked by those least in a position to know is to dumb down the gospel and to sell the needy short. It is to offer cheap grace. 'Our primary concern,' in Bloesch's words,

> is not with the probing questions of the culture but with the divine question that both judges and answers (cf. Job 40:7; 42:4). The gospel does not so much meet human needs as challenge and transform them. It makes

us more cognizant of our needs for salvation even while it often denies our immediate instinctive needs.[14]

Phil Kenneson and James Street ask if the contemporary evangelical church is itself a quotation of the culture or a question mark over the culture! They endorse Rene Padilla's judgment, that

> the missiology that the church needs today is not one that conceives of the people of God as a quotation taken from the surrounding society, but one that conceives it as an embodied question mark that challenges the values of the world.[15]

THE GOD WHO ANSWERS BY QUESTIONS

Before we look at each of the five questions in detail, let's pause to explore the reasons why God asks these particular questions of us. One thing is clear. It cannot surely be in order to make up a lack in His knowledge of the situation. In fact, God asks us questions not to find out what He doesn't know but to help us discover Him in a deeper way and to see ourselves in a truer light. 'The interrogative mood,' says Anthony Gittens, 'is capable of creating relationships, for the act of asking questions indicates a relationship with someone else outside ourselves.'[16] In inviting us to 'help Him with His inquiries', the Lord is not interrogating us but calling us to step into freedom with Him.

His questions are intended to draw us out, not to put us down. God is the Master Counsellor probing the fault lines of our soul. His questions shine a light on the twilight zone between soul and spirit. His queries gently invade our privacy not to expose but to heal. He patiently investigates the labyrinthine ways of the human heart not to increase His knowledge but to help us know ourselves better. He quizzes us not so that we can pass a test but so that we can embrace reality; not to catch us out but to call us into true self-knowledge.

In his prescient opening to the *Institutes of the Christian Religion*, more than three and a half centuries ago, John Calvin both anticipated and undermined our modern, psychological preoccupation with self-awareness. 'Nearly all the wisdom we possess, that is to say, true and sound wisdom, consists of two parts: the knowledge of God and of ourselves.' Hesitating for a moment as to which comes first, Calvin soon decides that 'it is certain that man never achieves a clear knowledge of himself unless he has first looked upon God's face, and then descends from contemplating him to scrutinise himself'.[17] So the One Creator God questions us not to elicit information but to restore us to just such a mutually revelatory relationship.

As we re-acquaint ourselves with 'the God Who asks questions', it is good to realise the great compliment Almighty God is paying us by questioning us as He does. God ennobles us by wanting our answer. He pays tribute to our human dignity by expecting us to be accountable. It has been said that the Greeks defined humans as rational beings. But the Bible defines humans as responsive and responsible beings. As Heschel said, 'I am commanded, therefore I am.'[18]

No one discovered this more painfully and yet more gloriously than Job. Recall his story. Bereft of family, wealth and health, Job lives in the long anguish of unanswered questions. While his so-called friends talk *about* God in deferential tones, Job in agony and anguish talks *to* God. He bravely and rightly remains dissatisfied with the glib and clichéd answers his friends offer him. Job doggedly holds out for a bigger, final answer to his turmoil. He deserves more than his friends' conventional religious answers. As someone said, when life is a picnic we play at religion, when life is a tragedy we grope for a theology. This is just what Job does. The amazing thing is that when Job is finally 'face to face' with God, it is God who asks all the questions! Initially the Lord sounds overbearing and intimidating but His questions are meant to rouse Job from despair and defeat. In the very act of being questioned by the One Creator God, Job is being called to repent of his dust-and-ashes self-denigration. No suffering or injustice, however severe, can rob us of the dignity of our God-given humanness. God's questions summon Job to stand on his feet, to stand up and be counted once again as a responsive, responsible human being made in God's image for fellowship and partnership.

As our finest modern Christian troubadour, Michael Card, suggests: 'Could it be that questions tell us more than answers ever do?'[19] This is what Job discovered. God gives no answers because He is not the Answerer; God is Himself the Answer!

I agree with Christian philosopher Peter Kreeft when he says that this is

> the answer to everything. No one, not even Job, can ever be dissatisfied with this answer. No one will have any more questions when he sees this answer. No one will ever feel let down, cheated or disappointed with this answer, no matter how demanding and dissatisfied he is with everything else. This is the answer that fills the infinite, God-shaped vacuum that is the human heart. This is God.[20]

SOUL OR SELF?

There is one further important thing to note before we leave our introduction to God's questions. If it is divine love that prompts these questions, it is human sin that occasions them. We usually view the Garden of Eden as an idyllic paradise of innocence and perfection. This is misleading. Rather the Garden is a testing ground. There was innocence but it was untested innocence; there was perfection but it was a potential perfection, not a completed one. When the

Creator made space for His human creatures to occupy, there was the potential to walk closely with Him or to walk away from Him, to run to Him or run from Him, which is sin. The human couple knew limitation; they did not know or need to know everything. They needed divine revelation, and were called to live by trusting God's word. Anything else is sin. As under-managers of God's estate, they were given tasks and responsibilities for which they were liable and accountable. To squander God-given gifts in the service of self rather than God is sin. To have the capacity for fierce feelings of joy and to seek emotional wholeness outside of God's loving will – this too is sin.

Knowing loneliness, Adam was meant to find fulfilment in relationship with others whose significance would both limit and complement his humanity. To turn against wife or brother or friend is sin.

In biblical light, each of us is accountable before God. The demise of this sense of accountability is due, in part at least, to the *loss of the concept of 'soul'* in serious Christian theology. In fact, in recent decades, the psychological self-help industry has hijacked the idea of the 'soul'. Evacuated of its true transcendent dimension, it serves as a symbol for the sacred cow of individual self-identity. Much has been lost in this devaluation of meaning. In Philip Rieff's astute summary, 'Religious man was born to be saved; psychological man is born to be pleased. The 'triumph of the therapeutic' – to cite Rieff's oft-quoted prophetic phrase – means that 'How do I feel about that?' has long displaced 'How might God feel about that?' In a discussion of this, Jeffrey Boyd, who is both a theologian and a trained psychiatrist, makes a passionate plea for the reinstatement of the Christian concept of 'soul'. 'We want,' he urges,

> a word around which to rally. Without this single word
> – a single word that ordinary lay people understand – the
> average American will never understand why the self is
> intrinsically theological.

He points out that souls are accountable to God but selves are answerable finally only to themselves![21]

As Dietrich Bonhoeffer reminded us, Jesus never called people into their sin but out of their sin.[22] So He seldom answered the questions He was asked but usually recast them as questions of His own, turning them back on the questioners with gentle irony, inviting further thought, offering a wider perspective, probing for a deeper response, clearing the vision for a new view of reality, opening a door of perception and entry to the kingdom of God. Jesus was looking for those who were weak and poor and humble enough to determine to become disciples of the kingdom. 'Who stands fast?' Bonhoeffer asks.

26

Only the man whose final standard is not his reason, his principles, his conscience, his freedom, or his virtue, but who is ready to sacrifice all this when he is called to obedient and responsible action, who tries to make his whole life an answer to the question and call of God. Where are these responsible people?[23]

The pioneering Christian psychologist Paul Tournier endorses a comment of Jacques Ellul that to be responsible is to *have to* reply! Ellul recalls two of the first five great questions God puts to his human creatures.

In the response to the question 'Adam where are you?' lies the possibility of becoming a person; in responding to the question 'Where is your brother?' lies the road to personal relationships.[24]

Like many modern German theologians, Jürgen Moltmann has consciously carried out his work in the shadow of Auschwitz. He suggests that Auschwitz posed three questions. One, 'Is God dead?' If he isn't, he should be. Or if he isn't, second, why did he permit such horror? These questions, says Moltmann, receive no facile answers; they seek a suffering God if they seek God at all.

But then there is a third question, which we often suppress with the help of the first. It is God's question about men and women ... After Auschwitz, do we still have a human future worth living for? In this context we don't cry 'Where is God?' We hear the eternal voice which cries 'Adam, where are you?' and 'Cain, where is your brother?' and 'What have you done?'[25]

It is to these very questions that we turn now, to hear them addressed to us.

So soberly but without apprehension we can seek with T.S. Eliot to 'be prepared for the coming of Him who knows how to ask questions'.[26] It is with confidence that we can face God's first questions, believing them to be not the accusing inter-rogations of a judge but the entreaties of a loving Father.

Q1

'WHERE ARE YOU?'
(Genesis 3:9)

DAZED FROM A FALL IN MY GARDEN, I WAS LYING ON A trolley outside the Radiology Department of my local hospital. I had fallen off a ladder onto a concrete patio, so my field of vision had now been restricted by a neck-collar. But it was enough to allow me to read a poster on the wall above me. The poster warned pregnant women of the dangers posed by X-rays to their unborn children. It depicted a fetus calling out: 'Mummy, tell them I'm here!' My first thought was to wonder if the poster ever appeared in the reception lobby of abortion clinics. My second thought was to ponder: 'Does anyone know we're here? Is there anyone concerned about our whereabouts?'

Once dumb in the womb, one day dead in the tomb or, right now, damned as we all are by the Fall in the Garden, does anyone care where we are?

We may begin to find an answer to our question by tuning in to God's first question addressed to Adam and Eve: *'Where are you?'*

Again we remind ourselves that the Lord is not asking this question because He lacks knowledge of the couple's whereabouts. His question reflects His desire to repair the broken fellowship which they and He had enjoyed. Where once God and humans had walked closely together, sharing intimate companionship, now there was estrangement and distance. Unwilling to give up on the divine-human friend-

31

ship, the Lord asks this searching question.

I believe that this is the *theological* question foundational to everything else, which each of us should echo by asking: 'Where am I in relation to God?' In long experience of counselling and probing beneath the surface of every issue, almost invariably one comes on this deeper issue of the person's relationship with and attitude to God.

What the Bible reveals and experience confirms is that we are lost, alienated from the Father. We are cut off from our source of life, estranged from His love. We find ourselves homeless in an increasingly hostile environment. Such is the terrible effect of sin – only to be matched by the relentless love of a seeking God.

STIGMATA OF THE FALL

The couple's first reaction to their fractured relationship with God is to become aware for the first time of their nakedness. 'Then the eyes of both of them were opened, and they realised that they were naked' (Gen. 3:7). Sin makes them fear exposure. Security and trust having vanished, they now feel threatened and vulnerable. In von Rad's words, 'Fear and shame are henceforth the incurable stigmata of the Fall.'[1] Before the Fall, Adam and Eve were unashamed to recognise their nakedness (Gen. 2:25). Now the 'opening of their eyes' represents an awakening to shame.

It is important at this point to distinguish between healthy shame and unhealthy shame. Given the fallenness of our world, a capacity to sense shame was once regarded as a virtue. This healthy sense of shame has to do with respect for boundaries, one's own and that of others. It entails a mature self-awareness, an ability to anticipate the impact of my legitimate self-expression and to restrict its scope for your sake. This is not a matter of being psychologically inhibited. Inhibition is usually a self-protective mechanism. But to be self-controlled is lovingly other-protective. Here the self treads gently lest it treads on another's dreams and infringes another's space. To be capable of shame then is to be modest, as opposed to exhibitionist; to be restrained as opposed to being vulgar. It is a mark of character to be sensitive to social standards and the feelings of others.

Psychologists tell us that a benign sense of shame is necessary for our well-being. Shame tells us of our limits as humans. In James Bradshaw's words, 'Healthy shame is the psychological foundation for humility.'[2] By contrast, a total lack of shame – being *shameless* – is consistently condemned in Scripture. It means to indulge in inappropriate behaviour, to expose oneself flagrantly, to flaunt convention. Just before his death, the eminent US social commentator Christopher Lasch lamented the contemporary 'abolition of shame'. He noted with regret that the USA is being described as a 'cultureless society' because, as he puts it, 'It is a society in which nothing is sacred, nothing forbidden.' When

President Jimmy Carter admitted to the sin of lusting after a woman in his heart, he was universally derided; when President Bill Clinton blustered evasively that he 'did not have sex with that woman', he was widely and sniggeringly indulged. 'Moralists advise us,' notes Lasch,

> that words like 'outlandish', 'perverse', and 'degraded' belong to a discredited, excessively judgmental vocabulary of hierarchy and discrimination. The only thing forbidden in our culture of exposure is the inclination to forbid – to set limits on disclosure.[3]

After Bill Clinton addressed Britain's Labour Party conference, even the London *Times*' editorial was in uncharacteristically waspish mood when reflecting on his performance:

> The comeback kid became the throwback kid in a triumph for charm over credibility, revisionism over record and chutzpah over substance. And the audience loved it. They were not so much eating out of his hand as throwing their underwear at him. It was more Tom Jones than Thomas Jefferson. The USA once had founding fathers. It now has shameless sons.

And there, but for the grace of God, go all of us.

EMOTIONAL SELF-ABUSE

But what is equally if not more damaging emotionally and socially is to be *shameful*. This is that toxic sense of shame – first felt by Adam and Eve after sinning – which makes people feel unworthy, disgusting, rejected and self-condemned. It dissolves self-respect in the acid of self-loathing. Being shameful, says pastoral theologian Ray Anderson, amounts to 'emotional self-abuse'.[4]

Psychologist Robert Kaplan describes it as a 'repressed but hounding shame, something activated to the level of gnawing self-doubt, occasionally reaching the intensity of fully inflamed self-hatred.'[5] Kaplan argues that guilt is about doing, while shame is about being. 'We say, "I am ashamed of *myself*. I am guilty *for something*."'[6] This is, as David de Silva points out, an oversimplification, since we often feel ashamed of having done bad things and this is in fact a 'helpful safeguard against the dangers of sin'.[7] Either way, as Lewis Smedes puts it, 'Guilt overflows the banks of action and floods our being with shame.'[8] One wrong and isolated action can falsely freeze our view of ourselves as a thoroughly bad person. Undeserved shame exaggerates our faults, and hardens into a chronic condition, leaving us 'shame-bound'.[9] Especially vulnerable to toxic shame, says Smedes, are the overly responsible, the obsessive moralisers, the compulsive comparers, the approval addicts, the never-deserving – to which maybe added those crippled by bad memories, those who dwell in the shadow of their fathers or feel condemned by their dreams.[10] Unhealthy shame is summed up by Smedes, as 'a false feeling inflicted by the false ideals implanted in us by secular culture, graceless religion, and unaccepting parents'.[11] It is sin that does this, and God wants to save us from it. As an excuse for turning away from Him, it will not do.

'Are you going home for Christmas?' Christian Campus evangelist Jimmy Long asked Joan, a Christian student. She immediately burst into tears.'My parents divorced long ago, I don't have a home to go to, nowhere where I belong.' Joan, who knew her sins were forgiven, nevertheless confessed to being ashamed of her past and unable to accept herself as anything other than unworthy and disgraceful. Many of her generation – Generation X as it is styled – come from dysfunctional families and suffer a desperately low sense of self-worth. They innately hunger for acceptance and love. The gospel that Generation X particularly needs to hear, argues Jimmy Long, is the gospel of 'adoption out of shame into God's family'.

If we are going to minister faithfully within the emerging postmodern generation, our churches need to provide teaching and practical assistance to help this generation overcome its shame and realise adoption into God's family.[12]

But for this to happen, the Church needs to be a community where trust and honesty encourage confession of sins and hurts, and where forgiveness flows and love covers a multitude of sins. David de Silva suggests that the Church, like Alcoholics Anonymous, sees itself as 'sinners anonymous'.[13] Admitting our solidarity in sin, and experiencing real reconciliation with a holy God, removes the sense of being a shameful person through what we have done, and allows access to the real person behind the mask, who may stand in need of further healing and restoration. This is good news for all lost prodigals, young and old, who are still hiding away from a distant God. He wants you home and is asking still, 'Where are you?'

Naked and afraid they hid themselves. That says it all. The loving presence they had walked in as in a cool afternoon, as in a fragrant garden, as breathing fresh air – is a presence they have now withdrawn from. They no longer look at each other in the same way; they no longer look at God in the same way. That glorious face they had once rejoiced to see they now avert their eyes from. Fearful and embarrassed, they make the humorously futile attempt to hide from God! We all work hard at this silly game, don't we? We try to hide from the living God as much in respectability, careers, work and family life, as we do in pleasure, self-indulgence and hedonism.

Tragically and even more ludicrously many people seek to

take shelter from God in religion. In fact this is one of our last refuges from the living God! Karl Barth said that 'Adam, where are you?' becomes, especially for the theologian, the question 'How are things with your heart?' 'Are you,' he asked, addressing his fellow theologians,

> are you perhaps – in your private and interior life – fleeing from One with whom you as a theologian are pre-eminently concerned? Have you hidden from Him in the shrubbery of your more or less profound or high-flown contemplation, explication, meditation and application?[14]

When we turn away from the Creator, the apostle Paul argues, we do not automatically become unreligious; in fact, he says, we simply substitute for the real God idols of our own making. Idolatry is a favourite escape route. But as R.C. Sproul puts it, such 'religion is not the fruit of a zealous pursuit of God but the result of passionate flight from God'.[15]

Are you one of the Lord's people who hides from Him at times? The deep pit in which Gideon was beating out wheat in a wine-press to hide it from the marauding Midianites seems a symbolic hiding place from God for Gideon himself. Or so it seems from the story. Confronted by the challenge of God's call, he was, as we say, trying to keep his head down. Maybe he kept his head beneath the parapet of life through a sense of inferiority. 'How can I save Israel? My clan is the weakest in Manasseh, and I am the least in my family' (Judg. 6:15). The US humorist James Thurber has one of his famous animal cartoon characters peeping round a rock. This is the 'hippopoteramus' which, he said, 'almost never completely came out from behind anything'! Just like some fearful people.

And what about Elijah fleeing for his life from Ahab and Jezebel? Depressed and deflated after his greatest prophetic triumph, he wants to lie down and die! The prophet evidently shrinks from further demands upon his psychic and spiritual energy levels. God gently ministers to him through an angel, sound sleep and a good square meal until He finally gets his full and undivided attention and asks: 'What are you doing here, Elijah?'

As F.B. Meyer puts it in his usual winsome way,

> How often is that question still put? When a person who is endowed with great faculties digs a hole in the ground and buries the God-entrusted talent, and then stands idle all day, again the question must be asked; 'What doest thou here?'

'It may be', ponders Meyer,

> that these words will be read by those who have failed.

You once avowed yourselves to be the Lord's but all that is now over. You have fallen, as Milton's archangel, from heaven to hell. You have failed, and perhaps failed, as Elijah did, where you were expected to stand. And you are ashamed; you want to hide yourself from all who knew you in happier days; you have given up heart and hope. But remember; though forsaken by man, you are not forgotten of God. He loves you still, and waits beside you in order to restore your soul, and give you back the years that have been wasted.[16]

Think of Jonah trying to run away from God's call to go to Nineveh, by losing himself in the opposite direction! This too would be funny were it not so tragically true of us too. What failure of nerve or trust makes him run like this? Jonah takes ship to Tarshish to flee from God's calling. But even on a 'safe-passage' heading for the furthest point from God's will, even there just where you feel safe and out of sight, that quiet but persistent voice of Love will search you out and ask: 'Where are you?'

FAR COUNTRY

Perhaps the most famous of Jesus' parables illustrates the point perfectly. The younger of the two sons asserts his independence from his father, claims his share of the inheritance, and puts as much distance as he can between himself and his father's home.

There in that 'far country' he squanders what he has been given in self-indulgent and dissolute living. Having spent everything he is forced to take on work as a hired hand. Hungry and desperate, he even begins to covet the menu of the pigs he's looking after – surely the ultimate humiliation for a son in a Jewish story!

He is now a pathetic shadow of his once proud self. Shamed and vulnerable, he comes to his senses and wonders what on earth he's doing in the place. Turning his back on the father, he realises, has proved an illusory freedom. Lost in a blunderland of his own making, far from home in a strange country, alienated from the father by wrong choices, he finds himself in lonely exile. Resolved to return home, he's scarcely under way when he meets his father running towards him with outstretched arms. For an elderly Eastern man to tuck his cloak in his belt and start running would have been regarded as highly embarrassing. But the father is not ashamed to own his son and the son is too desperate to allow social niceties to stand in his way. Shame is overcome by unashamed grace. Scruffy and smelly in his humiliation, he is engulfed in an accepting embrace.

Remember: this is your God, so deeply driven by the longing to know where you are that He takes the initiative in coming to find each one of us. As C.S. Lewis memorably reflected: 'Amiable agnostics talk cheerfully about "man's search for God". To me, as I then was, they might as well

41

have talked about the mouse's search for the cat!'[17]

The story of the prodigal son expresses the plight of the people of Israel. For Israel was once acknowledged uniquely as God's 'son'. Israel was gifted with unique and wonderful privileges – the Presence of the Living God in saving wonders, in the living Word through the bond of covenant, and in glory in the Temple.

Israel, too like the errant son, had throughout its history continually opted to break loose from God and live as an independent power in the world of nations. Forever turning a deaf ear to the entreaties of the prophets, Israel ended up under the judgment of God, taken captive to Babylon. The people who believed they were God's own people now felt themselves to be cut off from their life-supply, exiles in a distant and alien country. The shame and humiliation of this plight is writ large in the Old Testament narrative and its pain expressed in many places notably, Lamentations and Psalm 137.

Back in the land for many centuries but with no end to the real exile from God yet experienced, Israel was divided in its reaction to Jesus' announcement of the end of exile, the day of forgiveness, the fulfilment of the prophets' hopes of salvation. The hard-nosed religious types were blind to the day dawning before their very eyes. But those who knew from bitter experience how exiled they were – the poor and sick, the sinner, tax-collectors and prostitutes – heard him gladly as good news. They turned right round and headed back to the Father's kingdom. It was to those who criticised this movement of the shamed and fearful out of their hiding place back to the full light of the Father that Jesus directed just such a parable as the parable of the two sons! Like the younger son, these lost prodigals found that repentance was not a condition for going home; it was going home!

OUT OF CIRCULATION

And this is everyone's story too. God asks us all, 'Where are you?' This is a universal condition of fallen humanity. We have all sinned, gone off like sheep astray, dropped out of divine circulation, losing our value like a lost coin. We have all gone missing from the Father. A long-estranged father is said to have posted a notice in a Spanish market square: 'Son, I've missed you and want you back: meet me in the square at noon on Friday.' And 87 young men turned up! As a world of sinners we are, the apostles tell us, alienated and cut off from God. We need to be reconciled to God.

But to be told you're lost is to be paid a strange compliment. It implies that you are valuable; it assumes that you belong somewhere and it strongly suggests that someone misses you and may well be looking for you! Not even a bad conscience can conceal this. Adam and Eve were called out of their shameful hiding place. God did not leave them to stew or even rot in their consciousness of guilt. With the

43

question 'Where are you?', says Bonhoeffer,

> the Creator calls Adam forth out of his conscience. Adam
> must stand before his creator. Man is not allowed to
> remain in his sin alone, God speaks to him, he stops him
> in his flight: 'Come out from your hiding place, from
> your self-reproach, your covering, your secrecy, your
> self-torment, your vain remorse ... do not lose yourself
> in religious despair ... stand before your Creator.[18]

God did not expose their nakedness and put them on
display in scornful judgment. Remarkably, says the text of
Genesis, 'God made garments of skin for Adam and his wife
and clothed them' (Gen. 3:22). In R.C. Sproul's words,
'Beneath the gaze of God Adam found redemption, not
annihilation. Adam experienced not only the stare of
judgment but the benevolent gaze of love.'[19]

THE ARMS OF THE CRUCIFIED

And it is the death of the 'eldest son' on the cross that
reconciles all God's lost children to the Father's heart and
restores them to His house. 'The God of the gospel',
observes Tom Smail,

> is even more gracious than the God of the parable; he does
> not just wait and long for us to come back to him, he sends
> his Son who is one with himself to the far country of
> Calvary to do what needs to be done to bring us home.[20]

In Miroslav Volf's words, 'The arms of the crucified are open – a sign of a space in God's self and an invitation for the enemy to come in.'[21] For us Jesus endures the cross, 'despising its shame'. With her sister Betsie, forced to strip naked in front of leering Nazi guards, Corrie ten Boom realised, she writes, 'that Jesus had hung naked on the cross'. The artists of the great Renaissance paintings of the crucifixion reverently added at least a scrap of cloth. But it was not like that, Corrie realises, on the first Good Friday. 'I leaned towards Betsie,' she recalls,

> ahead of me in the line. Her shoulder blades stood out sharp and thin beneath her blue-mottled skin. 'Betsie, they took his clothes too'. Ahead of me I heard a little gasp. 'Oh Corrie. And I never thanked him …'[22]

So through a Jesus crucified, shamed and exposed, the Father welcomes us in, enfolding our shame and nakedness in His grace, covering our sins with His Son's blood, clothing us in a new righteousness and putting a ring of belonging on our finger. Reconciliation includes forgiveness but is more. God not only addresses our guilt but He absolves our disgrace, and reinstates us in the feasting and festivity of the Father's kingdom. 'Today you shall be with me in paradise.' So, as Richard John Neuhaus reminds us, 'The first one home is a thief.'[23]

If I take the wings of the morning and find myself lost in

the dark night of the soul, crippled by self-destructive behaviour, will that searching voice still reach me and urge me to come out into the light?

If I make my bed in hell, will He find me there and enable me to say, as He miraculously enabled Betsie ten Boom to say to her sister, Corrie, in Ravensbruck, 'No pit is so deep that he is not deeper still'?[24]

And if I make my own bed and lie on it in a hell of my own self-loathing, will the loving entreaty follow me still into the suicidal darkness to ask, 'Where are you?'

By the cross of His Son, the God Who asks 'Where are you?' comes to wherever we are to seek and to save that which was lost and to bring them home.

> Come, ye weary, heavy-laden,
> Bruised and ruined by the fall;
> If you tarry till you're better
> You will never come at all …[25]

Dazed and damned, as all of us are by the Fall in the Garden, do we hear the searching Voice, 'Where are you?' More to the point, do we want to be found and to follow that Voice wherever it may take us?

'WHO TOLD YOU?'

(Genesis 3:11)

I REALISE AS I WRITE THESE WORDS ON MY E-MAIL-Internet-connected PC that my life has spanned a media revolution. As a small boy, I remember pressing my ear to our new 'steam-radio', only in those far-off post-World War II days, we called it simply 'the wireless'. It sat atop our sideboard and was a Bakelite beauty whose bulbous glass valves when lit glowed through the walnut fretwork. Listening, if not easy, was eagerly attempted. It was tuning-in that was deucedly difficult. My father twiddled the knobs and we trawled the crackling airwaves ... Hilversum, Daventry, Cologne ... everywhere but our desired station, the BBC Home Service. I was fascinated and frustrated by the medley of foreign voices from mysterious places. It was as if we had tuned in to the Tower of Babel.

'We are,' says Will Willimon, 'the only listeners God's got!'[1] If he's right then we have quite a responsibility. Can we find the wavelength God is broadcasting on? And when we do, have we got ears to hear?

For the Bible-based faith of both Jews and Christians, everything is predicated on the fact that 'God has spoken'. This is the astounding foundation of all we profess to know and believe; that the One Creator God has broken the eternal silence and spoken to us! One Rabbi is reputed to have been so overwhelmed by this one fact that in a lifelong teaching ministry he never progressed beyond the words '... and God said ...'

Yet from the start the Bible recognises that the cultural airwaves are crowded with competing truth-claims, which clamour for our allegiance. Now, as then, we need to reckon with the second of the questions that God asks: *'Who told you ... ?'* In asking this, it seems the Lord is seeking to expose the process by which Adam has come to realise his nakedness and be ashamed in the presence of his wife and of God. We might surmise that it was Adam's conscience, seared by sin, that made him so morally embarrassed. But no immediate answer is forthcoming. Instead Adam seeks to avert the question by off-loading the blame to Eve: 'She gave me some fruit from the tree and I ate it.'

But the question will not go away so easily. In fact it hangs over the whole sorry story. If 'Where are you?' was the great theological question, 'Who told you?' is the great *ideological* question. It is the great *truth* question. It asks: Where did your ideas come from? Who convinced you to think like that? What forces or influences have conditioned you to entertain those thoughts? What voices are you listening to that are shaping the course of your life?

We must be careful how we read the text here lest we shift the blame to the devil: 'The devil made me do it'! In the Genesis story, it is not the devil as later theology describes him but the serpent who is the source of untruth. It is all too easy to feel we are overwhelmed by supernatural forces in yielding to falsehood. But in the story before us it is no supernatural power but another creature that leads the humans astray. This is a way of saying that the lies come from within the created order. We are susceptible to them; we don't need an extraterrestrial power to explain why we believe them! What happens here is not the result of an eternal cosmic dualism between two equally powerful forces: God and Satan. Evil gains a foothold in us only by human permission! It will eventually be exposed and defeated on this same earthly stage only by the Last Adam's truthfulness and obedience. When He comes on the scene then the father of lies will truly be revealed as behind it all.

It is salutary to note, then, that lies and falsehood spring from within the created order and are not introduced to it by some supernatural power that is equal with God. In fact the serpent is described only as 'crafty'. But this craftiness is enough to bring about our human downfall. Think first of what we might call his intellectual craftiness. The serpent quotes God's prohibition but subtly overstates it by adding 'any tree' to the one tree they are banned from using (Gen. 3:1). What this does is raise unnecessary doubt in Eve's mind about what exactly God had said.

MENTAL QUALITY CONTROL
Once more we need to differentiate between healthy and unhealthy doubt. Honest doubt is a mark of a healthy mind and is to be commended. Honest doubt is our mental

quality control, which saves us from being gullible. The much-admired Christian writer, Flannery O'Connor once wrote to a student friend facing intellectual challenges to his faith. She advised him not to passively soak up the received secular wisdom of his university teachers. She commended a particular author to him as able to provide not answers but different questions. 'What kept me a sceptic in college,' she wrote, 'was precisely my Christian faith. It always said: wait, don't bite on this, get a wider picture, continue to read.'[2]

It is cynical doubt that is damaging and self-destructive. The modern world was built on the seventeenth-century philosopher Descartes's dictum: 'I think, therefore I am.' This crowned human reason as king. Only what can be rationally explained and intellectually mastered is adjudged as real and valid. In fact Descartes really said: 'I doubt, therefore I am' and once that process started it would surely end in tears. Modern man doubts everything. Taken to its logical end, such an attitude dissolves truth in an acid bath of scepticism and despair. We wonder if there is any true word from beyond ourselves on which we can rely. Sadly, when God speaks, instead of submitting to His word we stand in judgment on it.

Then there is the serpent's common-sense craftiness. 'You will not surely die' (v. 4)! This is the voice of the ordinary person in the street. 'Surely that can't be the case. Surely God didn't say that. I simply don't believe that will happen.' This turns out to be a flat contradiction of God's Word. It makes God a liar! But often it is more subtle than that. We might even talk of the serpent's religious craftiness! The serpent pretends to a privileged and exclusive insight into what God knows and thinks and to have an insider track on what God's real intentions are. Here is a beguiling voice, which offers a deeper insight into God's motives. It suggests that God's command not to eat of the tree of the knowledge of good and evil shows God up as a God Who is not good, Who is not out for our best interests, Who is withholding from us a wisdom that would threaten His position if He allowed us access to it! What presumption! As Bonhoeffer said, 'The serpent claims to know more about God than man, who depends on God's word alone.'[3] Beware Greeks bearing gifts of superior gnosis and mystical understanding not available to the plain person who hears God's voice.

The temptation to eat of the tree of good and evil was precisely the modern temptation to construct morality apart from God, to construe our own structure of what is right and wrong independent of a loving and trustful relationship with our Creator. 'The man and the woman,' in Derek Kidner's perceptive words, 'have been sold a false idea of evil, as something beyond good; of wisdom, as sophistication; and ... of greatness, as greed.'[4]

IDEAS HAVE CONSEQUENCES
The truth question, 'Who told you ...?' therefore, reminds us

that, for good or ill, ideas have consequences. The historian Jonathan Glover points out that while private lies do limited damage, public lying is deadly when done by states that dispense with objective truth and the rule of law based on objective evidence and impartial testimony.

'In an authoritarian society,' he writes, 'there is much more power to defend the small lie by massively churning out the larger one. It is like printing money to get out of a financial crisis.'[5] What poisonous ideas first festered in the minds of the pioneers of Nazism? The great Jewish thinker Abraham Heschel reflected on the fate of his people and said: 'Instilled with the gospel that truth is mere advantage and reverence weakness, people succumbed to the bigger advantage of a lie – "the Jew is our misfortune"'. Heschel goes on: 'The roar of bombers over Rotterdam, Warsaw, London, was but the echo of thoughts bred for years by individual brains, and later applauded by entire nations'.[6] The psychiatrist Leo Alexander, who led the US Medical team at the Nuremberg Trials, explained that 'It all began when it was believed that there was such a thing as a life not worthy to be lived.'[7] Ruthless experiments in social engineering resulted. As in the case of Stalin and Mao, explains Jonathan Glover,

> It was thought acceptable to destroy things people valued, such as family, religion and the traditional culture. It was thought justifiable to kill so many and to

put such pressure on those left alive. The belief was that these things would further the Revolution, which in turn would produce a 'state overflowing with harmony and happiness'.[8]

Thankfully, it works the other way too. Václav Havel, the Czech President, said that what enabled him and his friends to survive under Communism and eventually overthrow its oppressive system was that the Soviet regime was governed by lies and propaganda, while Havel and his fellow freedom-lovers determined always to tell the truth and live by it come what might! Against that the Soviet system had no defence. As Solzhenitsyn said, 'One word of truth outweighs the whole world'.[9]

And consider the ideology that is shaping society in the UK today. The atheistic social commentator Polly Toynbee recently, and rightly, bemoaned the fact that the UK has the highest rate of teenage pregnancies in Europe. 'It's not just a matter of handing out more contraceptives,' she wrote, 'but of changing the ideas in young girls' heads.' I agree. But when it came to what those ideas might be she had nothing to offer, falling back instead on handing out the morning-after pill and making abortions more readily available! How pathetic and tragic. The root of the problem, as Toynbee sees, is precisely the ideas that feckless young girls have imbibed with their own mothers' milk.[10] Who told them the tragic untruth that freedom was gained by selfishness? What voice convinced them that pleasure-seeking was life's only goal? Who sold them this horrible lie about what it means to be a woman and a free and fulfilled human being? Was it perhaps intellectuals just like Ms Toynbee and her kind? The resultant hopelessness and blighted lives cry out for a gospel, for the light of truth in the darkness, for the voice of the Good Shepherd who leads out of the barren wasteland of despair into the rich pastures of abundant life.

TRUTH SUPPRESSED

Paul summarised our whole sinful predicament as believing a lie (see Rom. 1:25). Ideas do have consequences. The lie leads to a sliding scale of disaster. Due to sin, Paul says, we suppress the truth. In other words we sense what's true but we don't respond. We return from holiday in the Swiss Alps with our camera full of magnificent awesome scenery. But we do not come back to give thanks to the Creator for His creation. We have glimpsed the truth behind the splendour, we have heard the sound of His voice in the garden of beauty but we don't answer Him with gratitude and praise. Instead we 'suppress' the truth. We push it down into our subconscious. We bury it under the need to get on with our own lives, we smother it with work and family and career and business. Perhaps we fear this God would demand too much of us and so we divert our worship to gods of our own making. Another voice tells us that self-made gods are far easier gods to live with. We manufacture idols; we swap the real thing for substitutes. The consequences of suppressing the truth about God as our Creator are disastrous. The whole created order gets inverted and eventually perverted. We worship the creature, not the Creator.

Ceasing to love God, Narcissus-like, we fall in love with our own reflection, ending up with the ultimate form of self-love, which is homoerotic relationships and behaviour! Such people 'know perfectly well they're spitting in God's face. And they don't care – worse, they handout prizes to those who do the worst things best!' (Rom. 1: 32, *The Message*). How tragic, pitiful and cruel is a society that has believed a lie. The Father's heartfelt question burns with His own passion for a lost and damaged world:'Who told you?' Somehow through the airwaves cluttered with the lying voices that bombard us daily, we can perhaps detect the herald's voice announcing the gospel of truth, which is the power of God to save.

SLOW RUSTINGS OF SHAME

At a personal level, think of the voices you have listened to that have blighted you life. Maybe it was a teacher at school who sowed in you a permanent sense of shame? Does that voice still ring in your head that tells you: 'You're nothing ... You're useless ... You're no good for anything ... You'll never make anything of yourself'? That formative voice told you that you were wasted space and those words have burned deep into your hidden self, there to work their deadly poison on your self-respect. The jug-eared British comedian Lee Evans developed his rubber-faced and silly-walk comedy routine as a defence mechanism after being bullied at school. 'I was the only one in the class,' he admitted, 'not to pass a test. The teacher hauled me to the front of everyone and said: "Look at Lee. That's what failure looks like"!' Michael O'Siadhail confesses that he will often 'strum the chord of assurance' that an encouraging teacher strung for him. Many years later he recalls,

> I probe the essence of his energy
> no blandishments or bland approval
> his unblinking trust enticed me,
> fingered some awareness of worth
> in his praise all is possible.

Then the affirmation was swept away by the new broom of a replacement teacher from whose disparagement the poet learned only 'the slow rustings of shame'.[11]

Perhaps too you are a victim of damaging parental programming? The novelist Franz Kafka once wrote to his father: 'I was a mere nothing to you ... in front of you I lost my self-confidence and exchanged it for an infinite sense of guilt.' What did your parents want you to be when you grew up? 'We want you to be good' – how awful – thus reinforcing that dutiful striving to please everyone, that 'I-must-conform' mentality, so that all your life you have lapsed into guilt at not measuring up and a perpetual sense of failure. 'We want you to be successful' – which perhaps helps to explain why you are such a driven person, so ruthless, so competitive, so demanding on yourself and on others. This helps explain why A-level students are now committing suicide because they can't stand the pressure of living up to expectations. 'We want you to be happy' – this is, perhaps, the worst voice of all to listen to. It's a cheap and easy parental get-out. It offers no moral vision for living but is a recipe for self-centred pleasure-seeking that may as well be satisfied by robbing banks or paeodophilia! You are blessed indeed, as I am, if your parents said, feebly and blunderingly and in their own way, as mine did: 'We want you to be a lover of God!' They tried to ensure that the deepest voice I would always hear in my head would be the original voice of our Fatherly Creator saying:

> You are made in My image. I delegate My kingdom rule to you. I want you to be My partner in ordering the world. I have blessed you with individuality, with unique gifts and skills and creativity so that you can bless others. I give you the honour of bearing My image wherever you go. You have the dignity of being My son, My daughter. I love you unconditionally.

WHOSE MOUTHPIECE?
Let's stay on the domestic front and consider the perplexing fact that Adam was fooled into disobeying God

because he listened to his wife (Gen. 3:17)! This is a tough one. Surely, we want to query this. Surely, it's a good thing to listen to your wife. Would that every husband paid more sensitive attention to his wife, had more regard for her feelings, was considerate towards her views and opinions as a genuine conversation partner. Of course, but this narrative is not condoning insensitive relational deafness. Rather it is indicting a man for his moral weakness in allowing his wife rather than God to dictate to him his major moral moves.

I remember being a young pastor facing a strong and vociferous deacon in a deacons' meeting, knowing that he was merely the mouthpiece for his discontented and trouble-making wife back home. There are moral choices that only we can make. The voice of truth speaks to us and we can't hide behind someone else's opinion in answering it. It is our privilege to be addressed by God and we are answerable.

And think again of Job's story. With friends like Job's who needs enemies? They bombarded Job's bewildered mind with clichés and slogans. It was no comfort to know that they got their ammunition from Scripture. They were perverse alchemists, turning gold into dross. Job's friends managed to turn the healing proverbs of Lady Wisdom into the lacerating dogmas of what sounds like an 'omnipotent mother'.[12]

The question 'who told you?' was asked of Israel. Israel was unique in hearing God speak to them as no other people had, and was urged to live not by bread alone but by every word that came from God. The sad story of the Old Testament is of a people cast into exile for refusing to listen to the voice of God or to pay attention to his prophets. Jeremiah wrote Israel's epitaph: 'Truth has perished; it has vanished from their lips' (Jer. 7:28). Of course Israel had been ill-served by her leaders and kings. Think of how Aaron failed to follow God in leading God's people. When the children of Israel grew discontented with Moses and by implication with God, they made an idolatrous golden calf, aided and abetted by Aaron. When challenged by Moses, Aaron tried to excuse himself by saying that the people made him do it (Exod. 32). When Saul disobeyed God and Samuel asked him why, he admitted he had feared the people and listened to their voice (1 Sam. 15:24). These two were ahead of their time.

Too many of today's politicians do the same, leading by focus groups, making policy by Gallup poll, bending convictions according to how popular they might be. It was Groucho Marx who said: 'I have my principles but if you don't like them, I have others ...!' Think of the shifting, evasiveness during the Monika Lewinsky affair of President Bill Clinton, described by one scholar as 'the most skillful liar in American presidential history' and immortalised in a bumper sticker as 'Bill Clinton 99% fact-free!' How sad this is. How the nation suffers when truth and righteousness are not forming godly leaders and people.

THE BIG LIE

Let's ask this question, 'Who told you?' to the prodigal son in
Jesus' story. Who told the prodigal that he would best fulfil
his potential as a human being by turning his back on the
father who had given him birth and loved him? Who told him
that freedom was best achieved by breaking free of the
father's house and heart and going off to 'do your own
thing'? Biblical scholars tell us that by asking for his share of
the inheritance while his father was still alive, the son was
in effect wishing his father dead!

At what point did so many people in the modern world
begin to believe the lie that they would be better off if God
was dead? As theologian Stanley Hauerwas puts it: 'Who
convinced us that the only story worth having is a story we
chose to make up ourselves when we had no story?'[13] And
even when the prodigal comes to his senses, where did he
get the false idea that the only reception his father would give
him would be the grudging acceptance as a hired hand
rather than the full welcome of a returning son? Who told us
lies about God's goodness and grace? Who led us into
thinking God was mean and ugly and vengeful? Where did
we get those ideas from? Who convinced the older brother
that serving dutifully was all the father wanted, that the
father wasn't really interested in blessing him above the
course of duty, that the father was really withholding the best

from him and preferred keeping his nose to the religious grindstone? What made the son think the father so mean and ungenerous that it wouldn't be worth asking him for anything? By now we surely know and can tune the ears of our heart to another wavelength.

'Hear my voice when I call, O LORD', says the psalmist.

> Be merciful to me and answer me.
> My heart says of you, 'Seek his face!'
> Your face, LORD, I will seek.
> Do not hide your face from me ...
> Though my father and mother forsake me,
> the LORD will receive me.
>
> (Psa. 27:7–10)

Where we needed the assuring voice of father and the accepting smile of mother, we were offered the frowning disapproval of father and the nagging voice of mother. And sin even distorts the face and voice of our Divine Parent for us.

The much respected US church historian Roberta Bondi movingly recounts how, as a young girl, she confused her heavenly Father with her stern and unbending earthly father who tolerated no imperfections or weakness and allowed no arguing with him or asking 'Why?', especially from his wife and daughter! 'And if this was true of my

63

earthly father,' Bondi reasoned, 'how much more must this be the case with my heavenly Father. Surely my heavenly Father's standards for females had to be stricter than my earthly father's.'[14] She confesses that her attempts at saying 'Our Father' in public prayer regularly induced in her 'a sense of inadequacy, helplessness, and depression'. Thankfully, here is one feminist theologian who didn't jettison God the Father for some 'goddess' substitute. She found help in her own expertise, church history. Through reading the desert fathers – the medieval monks and mystics who lived close to God in the desert – Bondi rediscovered a God whose fatherliness embraced cast-offs and was gentle and gracious towards the weak. 'Could God the Father really expect less of me than my earthly father? Could God the Father want and even like women the church I knew rejected?' Bondi discovered, she writes, that to name God as 'Father' in prayer 'is to invoke God's fatherhood as a mighty corrective against all the murderous images of fallen fatherhood that hold our hearts and persons, our churches and our world captive'.[15] It is well worth saying that Roberta Bondi was led to draw near to her earthly father in the closing stages of his life and to enjoy a belated but deep friendship with him.

'But,' says the Lord, 'who told you that I was no better than your earthly father?' And who sold Lewis Smedes the lie that made him confuse God with his mother? Smedes, one of evangelicalism's best-loved wise men, tells of his lifelong struggles with the accusing voice. On a solitary spiritual retreat, he graphically describes how this battle came to a head.

I know it can be hell to be left dangling in the winds – without mother's milk of moral affirmation, no applause, no reinforcement, no support – only yourself. I got more and more nervous about the gap between the doctrine of grace computed into my cerebral cortex and my secret fantasy of earning God's approval by being a fine Christian fellow. I needed someone's pat on the head, somebody's stroking, somebody's clapping; I couldn't be sure of God's approval unless I got it from people around me. I had in fact, gotten my mother confused with God: I needed her approval, when you came right down to it, as much as I needed God's ... For me the boy inside was just a rotten kid who knew he had to be something better than he was in order to get mother's or God's – the two were never separated – approval. It was as if my mother was saying: 'I can never give you my approval after all, never, not ever. You are not, and never will be, good enough for me to love you.' I had never known such lonely pain, never such fear, never such helplessness, never such despair. I was lost, utterly lost. I felt a life of pious trying going down the drain, a life of half-baked belief in grace exposed as futile … I lay down in my spiritual waste. But I did not sink. When I flopped into nothingness, I fell into God … I fell into the hands of the living God. And 'God's hands are pierced with nails from Christ's cross, his hands are the strength of his love, the power to hold us and keep us from falling into a hell without God.'

Afterwards, Smedes recalls with immense relief,

I thanked him that with him I did not need to be good enough. I could flourish without my mother's approval … I thanked him that he was there to accept me 'without one plea but that thy blood was shed for me' … I felt love, so I knew I felt God. Or was it the other way around? … No matter. I felt it was right with me when everything was all wrong.[16]

RELIABLE REALITY

So in asking us the question 'Who told you?' a loving God is gently probing our confusion. He is seeking to gain a hearing with us. He queries whether we are listening too much to the opinion-formers in the media; whether we are bowing too easily to peer pressure or fashionable trends in our culture: whether we are paying too much attention to those damning and damaging voices from the past that echo through our memory. This question challenges the ideas we base our lives on lest we have believed a lie.

The Hebrew concept of truth is linked to faithfulness in making promises and keeping commitments; the Greek notion of truth contrasts the real and the illusory. Biblically, then, in short, truth is *reliable reality*. God is truth. God may be trusted because He is the True One. He is true, He acts true, He speaks truly. His word inscribed in the Bible is tried and tested and utterly trustworthy. We can read the Bible in this way. I like what the great theologian James Denney once said of his friend J.P. Struthers: 'He never reads Scripture as if he had written it but as if he were listening for a voice.'

Jesus Who embodies God's Word is truth in person. His words are words of eternal life. To become His disciple is to know the truth and the truth will set us free. The Holy Spirit is the Spirit of truth who leads us into the truth about Jesus. He creates a climate of reliable reality, not virtual reality, where we can be liberated from confusion, lies, propaganda and above all, self-deception. By hearing and holding to the truth as He tells it, we are set free to be lovingly truthful parents, teachers and friends. Within the fellowship of believers, we learn the truth as it is in Jesus and so are freed to speak truthfully in love to one another. And the truth is grace and acceptance.

To paraphrase a famous theologian, P.T. Forsyth, it has cost us much to find our way thus far. And we have yet a long way to go. But we believe we have found the true and magnetic North. And a voice is ringing in our ears: 'Follow me ...' He who has ears to hear, let him hear!

I studied at Spurgeon's College under the shadow of the BBC's giant radio transmitter on the top of Norwood Hill in South London. Our college motto was the great Victorian preacher's own personal 'coat of arms'. It showed a hand grasping a cross with the Latin tag *et teneo et teneor* – hold fast to the cross and be held fast by the cross!

The cross on the hill broadcasts the decisive message. 'Father, forgive them for they *don't know* what they are doing!' How can any of us fully anticipate the costly consequences of godless ideas? Whose idea was it to crucify Jesus? Did any of them know, really know what they were doing? Did Caiaphas, Pilate, the soldiers know? Does any of us know what finally comes from following an alien voice? They 'did not know' the scale, enormity and significance of what they were doing that day.

'I didn't know about the death-camps,' Hitler's close advisor, Albert Speer is reputed to have said, 'but I could have found out'!

No sin is trivial. Ideas do have fateful consequences. Passive indifference reaps a grim harvest. As was later ruefully said, 'They came for the mentally defective and I didn't protest; they came for the Jews and I didn't protest … then they came for me and there was no one left to protest …'

We didn't know it would come to this! But then it is sin's self-deception that blinds us to the fact that we are deceived.

THE MESSAGE OF THE CROSS

But the cross tells us the truth, about ourselves and about God. It shatters all distorted views of humanity and all twisted views of God. The cross reveals the paradoxical glory of a God Who in Christ achieves His greatest triumph over sin, evil and death through humiliation, vulnerability and death. The cross tells us that 'victory remains with love for He, our Lord is crucified'.[17] The cross tells us of God's settled determination to subvert all human wisdom and to save the world by the foolishness of a crucified Messiah, to overturn the love of power with the power of love.

In a world where the seeming lottery of random tragedy and injustice militates against believing in a caring God, the cross proclaims with blood-stained credibility the evidence of a God who took the risk of creating the world because He knew He had the sacrificial energy to redeem it.

> Inscribed upon the cross we see
> In shining letters 'God is love'.
>
> Thomas Kelly

'Herein is love, not that we loved God, but that he loved us, and sent his Son to be the propitiation for our sins' (1 John 4:10, AV). Putting our ear close to the ground at the foot of the cross we can hear him say, 'Father, forgive them, for they really were deceived about what they were doing.'

Who told you God was grudging and mean? It's a lie. If God did not spare His only Son but gave Him up for us all how will He not with Him freely give us all things?

Who told you that you were worthless? You are valued by the blood of Jesus Christ. If you were not worthy of His death for you, you were worth dying for! He paid a price for you. Having done so much, He cannot love you more, and He can never love you less. He aims to redeem you and to bring you into the fullness of your intended value.

The cross speaks the truth to those who have ears to hear and believe. This is the truth that sets us as free as love can make us.

Q3

'WHAT HAVE YOU DONE?'
(Genesis 3:13)

I STILL HAVE THE SCARS TO PROVE IT. I HAD DISOBEYED my mother's strict instructions and crossed the railway lines to ride my bicycle up a forbidden dirt track. I fell off. Yes, I know what you're thinking: he's been falling off things all his life! Well, I admit there is a lot about my fallenness in this book. On this occasion, I blamed the potholes in the road. But whatever the reason for my fall, I badly gashed my right elbow. I turned for home hoping that my mother's pity at my wounds would override her wrath at my wilfulness. It worked. But to this day, five decades on, a fragment of grey gravel stays embedded in my arm to remind me of what I did on that faraway summer afternoon.

Which sets me thinking on the larger human scale about the third question God asks after the Fall – in this case particularly directed to Eve. *'What is this you have done?'* (Gen. 3:13). This is the essential moral question addressed to each one of us. Life is a gift from God. What have I done with it? God holds me responsible for my actions and reactions. To realise this is both wonderful and frightening. Let me explain. One amazing privilege of being made in the image of God is that our choices count. We have been made to do things that – like God's actions – make a real difference in the world. Making decisions is part of our high and holy human dignity. I am not a speck of dust aimlessly floating through the cosmos. What I think and decide and do actually counts for something in God's world. But the corollary to this is sobering and challenging.

73

If my choices and actions are meaningful then I am responsible for them and will be held accountable for them. Our recovery from sin, therefore, as Lewis Smedes so well describes it, begins when we are willing to 'own our own stories',[1] when each of us learns to say: 'I did that. I was there. I take responsibility. I am the sort of person who is capable of doing that.' So we see that God's question, 'What have you done?' is a vital one if we are to begin to discover the true ethical basis to living.

As we continue to probe the essential ethical question God asks each of us, it is salutary to note how vividly the Genesis narrative highlights the tragic results of human sinfulness. We are shown the couple's sadly abject fear of God, their unhealthy shame in each other's presence, their tragic alienation from the natural world around them. We see close-up how desperately they try to hide from God, how futile is their quest to escape from God, how pathetic their attempt to cover up, how uneasy their concealment. In Ravi Zacharias's words, 'neither Adam nor Eve could break free from the ensuing anguish of a choice made in willful violation of God's command'.[2] And before we know it we are looking in a mirror. We spot the tell-tale signs of those evasive tactics we employ to avoid facing the awkward questions about ourselves. We recognise ruefully the self-defence mechanisms that we, too, erect to keep reality at bay.

CAUGHT IN THE HEADLIGHTS

People try to evade God's question in many ways. In today's world, the sophisticated and worldly-wise scarcely stop to listen to the question. If, in an unguarded moment, they faintly hear it, they usually laugh the whole thing off. The whole idea of moral responsibility is mockingly regarded as a relic of a medieval or Victorian mindset, depending on which historical age is the latest fall guy! This is something modern people see themselves as emancipated from. Hence the flagrant shamelessness that so often characterises public sin. Even worse than what is done is the way it is condoned and even applauded.

Paul brilliantly exposed the results of rebellion against God in his searing indictment in Romans 1. The perverted and depraved, the insolent and arrogant are all caught in the headlights of God's holiness. But, as we have already seen, special rebuke is reserved not for those who do such things but for all who positively approve of those who do! 'They know perfectly well they're spitting in God's face. And they don't care – worse, they hand out prizes to those who do the worst best!' (Rom. 1:32, *The Message*).

As Paul demonstrates, the inevitable outcome of rejecting God in favour of our own self-made idols is that we destroy our own humanity. In Peterson's paraphrase, 'refusing to know God, they soon didn't know how to be human either' (Rom. 1:26, *The Message*).

75

To evade God's question by denying His existence seems an easy balm for a troubled conscience. But when we eliminate God we diminish ourselves. Without His questioning love, we lose any sense of being made in the image of a personal Creator God. Slowly, more mechanistic views of human nature take over.

Even everyday speech betrays it. Once people would admit to having done wrong and say: 'I'm sorry, I was wrong.' Nowadays people mumble: 'I was out of order.' 'Out of order' – that's the notice we pin on a lift door when it isn't working! But what should we expect, when we view humans as mere machines, as bundles of electrical impulses? Then sin is redefined as a mere blip, a temporary fault, a loose connection. And how can I be held responsible for that? When we answer only to ourselves, we are dehumanised in the process.

TO OWE OR NOT TO OWE

Interestingly, then, we can detect two powerful but opposite tendencies at work in our contemporary world. On the one hand is the growing disinclination to feel any responsibility whatsoever; on the other hand we are overburdened with responsibility. Let's look at this paradoxical situation. First, and most obvious, is the widespread tendency to *avoid taking responsibility*. This leads to that 'victim-mentality' which is increasingly pervading everyday life. 'It wasn't my fault, nothing to do with me, these things happen.' Now of course we are all victims of life as well as active agents. Many people are genuine and innocent victims of abuse and violence. But what I am talking about is the glib psychologising of everything that happens. This is most readily apparent in the way we so readily offload the blame for what we have done. Adam blamed Eve. Eve blamed the serpent. And who put the snake there anyway? Eventually, once this process starts, God gets the blame – as is evident from Adam's emphasis on 'the woman you put here with me'. No doubt God was held responsible for making the tree too attractive in the first place!

So we blame our parents, our education or lack of it, the environment in which we grew up – too poor or too privileged – or we blame our spouse! The biological sciences now encourage us to blame it all on our genes. This blame-shifting accounts also for the increasing litigation that is paralysing relationships and working practices in the USA and increasingly elsewhere. Instinctively we know people should be held responsible but, since the notion is now discredited, we resort to psychology or law to compensate for the absence of a God-given moral basis to life. The gospel reveals that there is only one Scapegoat on Whom we can heap our sins and guilt and Who by His willing acceptance of them bears them all away.

Fewer and fewer people then seem willing to take

responsibility for their behaviour. But equally obvious is the opposite. There is a growing tendency to pile *too much responsibility* on to people. 'Taking responsibility' has become a buzzword. No longer am I to be held responsible for what lies within my sphere of influence but powerful voices are trying to make me feel responsible for saving the whales and rainforests too! We are being overburdened with obligations that few of us are directly implicated in. As a result more and more people are feeling powerless, numbed by the needs shown them, and convinced their choices amount to little. This too is a direct result of rejecting God and blocking out His searching question.

In Os Guinness's words,

> Modern responsibility, contradicting its origins, is all 'responsibility for' and 'no responsibility to.' Once we leave God out of the picture as the one to whom we are responsible, we succumb to the pressure groups that want to make us responsible for a great deal over which we have no direct control. This lays a crushing burden on us. We are told we are responsible for ourselves, for our bodies, for our futures, for our families, for our communities, for our environment, for our society, for the planet earth.

Yet, disastrously, says Guinness, 'We are not told to whom we are responsible for those burdens.'[3] No wonder so many people are overwhelmed and either become neurotic or throw off the idea of responsibility altogether. Better by far to come clean and walk towards the healing voice of our Divine Questioner and into His forgiving arms.

TRUE OR FALSE GUILT

Now, of course, for the sake of our own sanity and wholeness we must learn to distinguish true guilt from false guilt. False guilt is made up of feelings of emotional embarrassment. It is closely related to the unhealthy shame we discussed earlier. False guilt usually arises when we lose face as a result of our own failures. We then blame ourselves because the pain this causes punishes us for the dent in our own prideful self-image. Often what topples from its perch is not our true self but the idol we have set up of what we imagine ourselves to be. When the false self-image falls, false guilt ensues. Then again we may feel guilt wrongly because of expectations and obligations that are unfairly laid on us by others. This is a more common source of psychological damage, of which more later. But wherever false guilt comes from it is always in the end unhealthy.

True guilt is a recognition that I have offended God and infringed the high holiness of heaven. To confess this is tough and costly but life-giving. When he hid his sin and covered it up, the psalmist found that even the bones in his body paid the price (Ps. 32) and he felt as if he was wasting away. When he acknowledged his sin, he found health and blessedness. Where persistent and unjustified emotional embarrassment is a sign of incipient moral sickness, awareness of moral culpability is the first sign of regained health. Superficial remorse leads only to self-denigration and a slow death of genuine self-esteem; deep repentance is a godly sorrow that leads us back to God and through to life itself.

But what is that basic sin of which humans are guilty and for which they are morally accountable? Is disobeying God the cardinal crime committed here? Perhaps it is, if our first impression of the narrative is right. But if we probe a bit deeper we will see that it is not the original cause. Rather disobedience is a symptom of a profound lack of trust. Failure to trust God is the root problem that turns us away from God. Which is why turning towards God in repentance and faith is the first move we must make in receiving God's forgiveness and salvation. At the deepest level the couple have begun to doubt that God is good for them or out for their best interests. The suspicion has taken root in their minds that God intends to withhold from them what might be to their advantage. This anxiety is the first sign of that fear of death which is the root of all fear. What we fear most is loss of being. We fear any threat to our existence. This fear holds us in lifelong bondage. The shadow of a morbid anxiety looms over the valley of life.

The temptation to 'be as gods' and maybe achieve immortality and immunity from death drives us out of the arms of God and into the wasteland of mistrust. Our culture declares: 'Shame arises because I am a victim and I feel bad about myself.' The Bible declares: 'Shame arises because I am an idolater and I feel foolish when my idol topples.'[4] As theologian Ted Peters says,

> If we have faith in the God who created us and sustains us and cares for us, we will live with courage. We will become fearless in the face of harm and firm in the face of temptation. We will still have anxiety but it will not control our lives.[5]

But if we lose trust, our anxiety will overwhelm us and breed the sins that start with suspicion or gossip, and lead all the way up to theft and violence – all as a means of warding off threatening anxiety. And we subconsciously fear death because deep down our souls know that death is now not only a part of the natural order of things but also is most bitter for human beings because it is a judgment on our sin. Graciously God comes to ask the question 'What have you done?' not in the end to condemn but to make us face the reality of our predicament and to offer us His forgiveness with the perfect love that casts out fear, and the cross of Jesus that defeats the one who has the power of death, who is the devil.

AGAINST HEAVEN

Let's ask the prodigal the moral question: 'What have you done?'

The prodigal replies: 'I have sinned against heaven and in your sight.' He had wanted his father dead. He had believed the lie that striking out on his own and breaking with his father was the road to freedom. He had squandered his God-given gifts and talents. He had, as we say, 'got a life' but lost his soul. He had sold himself cheap to the commercial and entertainment interests in the culture.

What of the older brother in his religious self-righteous and dutiful serving? 'What is it he has done?': prided himself on keeping a clean sheet, accused his father of favouritism, failed to trust his father's goodness, refused to ask his father! He would much prefer a private dinner party with a few cronies to a public celebration of the joys of salvation. The younger son, coming to his senses, saw it all clearly: 'I have sinned against heaven and in your sight.' Did the older brother come to his senses too? The story doesn't say. But in any case the story of the two brothers is part of the bigger story of the Storyteller Himself, the Eldest Brother, who felt the Father's heart and left His Father's house to venture into a distant and alien country to seek and save the lost.

So by all means let us avoid 'guilt-tripping' and the false humility and mock modesty that go with it. Consider the rabbis who competed with each other in confession to be the most unworthy, only to be outdone by a third who repeated over and over again: 'I am a nobody, I am a nobody.' To which the only adequate reply was: 'Who does he think he is to be a nobody?'

Better to embrace the realism that refuses to exchange the language of sin for the language of therapy or victimisation. Let's not be squeamish by preferring the bland 'that saved a soul like me' to what John Newton wrote when he sang of the 'amazing grace that saved a wretch like me'. Let's avoid the evasion of claiming 'the devil' or 'my spouse' 'made me do it'. Don't blame your parents or your genes or your upbringing or your environment. Have the holy humour to reply as Chesterton did to a newspaper debate about what was wrong with the world. 'Dear Sirs, I am. Sincerely yours, G.K. Chesterton.'

Maybe 'I am the chief of sinners' sounds a bit presumptuous. In that case, leave such a confession to the apostle Paul. Content yourself to settle for the attitude of Father Neuhaus who writes:

> I may think it modesty when I draw back from declaring myself the chief of sinners, but it is more likely a failure of imagination. For what sinner should I speak of if not of myself ... About chief of sinners I don't know, but what I know about sinners I know chiefly about me.[6]

IT IS DONE!

Because Jesus trusted entirely to the Father even on the cross, we can trust again. We can 'trust in His trust'. The forgiveness that flows from the cross opens up a reliable future for us, for in the cross God proves beyond a shadow of doubt His faithfulness and love.

Violating God's moral law and character exposes me to real guilt, not self-remorse; and real wrath, not simply self-reproach. But the cross answers this perfectly by the forgiveness and non-condemnation it provides. When stung by unjust violence, we instinctively demand that 'something must be done … someone must pay'. At the cross we dare to believe that 'something has been done, and someone has paid'.

The Slain Lamb has become the Scapegoat who has paid the price. We need not shift the blame to others but can face our culpability and confess our sin.

What had Eve done? 'She took … and ate.' As Derek Kidner memorably said: 'So simple an act, so hard its undoing. God will taste poverty and death before "take and eat" become verbs of salvation.'[7] Because He did, our eating and drinking are no longer a sacrament of sin but a means of grace.

Leading churchman and poet John Donne needed and knew the grace of forgiveness, which he celebrated in a memorable poem – 'A Hymn to God the Father' – with its clever play on his own name at the end of each stanza.

> Wilt thou forgive that sin where I begun,
> Which is my sin, though it were done before?
> Wilt thou forgive those sins through which I run,
> And do them still, though still I do deplore?
>   When I have done, thou hast not done,
>   For I have more.
>
> Wilt thou forgive that sin by which I won
> Others to sin, and made their sin my door?
> Wilt thou forgive that sin which I did shun
> A year or two, but wallowed in a score?
>   When thou hast done, thou hast not done
>   For I have more.
>
> I have a sin of fear, that when I've spun
> My last thread, I shall perish on the shore;
> Swear by thyself that at my death thy sun
> Shall shine as it shines now, and heretofore;
>   And having done that, thou hast done,
>   I have no more.[8]

At the cross we can come home to the truth about what we have done and what God has done with what we have done.[9]

What have we done?

- We have sinned against heaven and in Your sight, Father.
- We have taken up arms as rebels against a holy God and transgressed His holy laws.
- We have fallen short of the mark of the glorious destiny planned for us, missing the 'the beauty of God's plan' (Rom. 3:23, J.B. Phillips).
- We have all been either sulking secret sinners or flagrant prodigals – and that includes those older brothers whose midlife madness prompts a late dash into prodigality.
- At one and the same time villains and victims of the piece, we have by turns overspent our credit or underspent our rightful inheritance, by turns refused or misused the gift of life.

Pilate's question to Jesus, 'What have you done?' echoes God's question to Adam and Eve[10] and evokes thoughts of Jesus Who, as 'the Second Adam, to the fight and rescue came'.

And what *has* Jesus done on God's behalf about what we have done?

- He has borne 'our sins in his body on the tree' (1 Pet. 2:24).
- He has died 'the righteous for the unrighteous, to bring [us] to God' (1 Pet. 3:18).

- He has been made 'a sacrifice of atonement, through faith in his blood' and 'reconciled' us to God (Rom. 3:25; 5:10).
- Through the eternal Spirit He has 'offered himself unblemished to God', to 'cleanse our consciences from acts that lead to death' and provided 'redemption through his blood, the forgiveness of sins' (Heb. 9:14; Eph. 1:7).

His saving work is finished; the debt is paid. In Tom Smail's words:

> The man who does right where everyone else is doing wrong is able, in the justice of God, to rescue us from all that is wrong and to give us a new beginning by breaking our relationship to sin and bringing us into a new relationship with God.[11]

So from the cross He can triumphantly say: 'It is accomplished: it is done!' What He has done to save us more than atones for what we have done. And for all eternity He has the scars to prove it.

Q4

'WHY ARE YOU ANGRY?'
(Genesis 4:6)

'ANGER IS PASSIONATE AGAINSTNESS.'[1] AND THERE ARE some things we should be passionately against – injustice, cruelty – in fact, sin in all its forms. Dan Allender and Tremper Longman III affirm that 'God designed and blessed anger in order to energise us to destroy sin'.[2]

'Anger,' said C.S. Lewis, 'is the fluid love bleeds when you cut it.'[3] When a toddler suddenly rushes out onto a busy road, who reacts more angrily, the mother or a passer-by?

There would be something wrong with us if we stayed passion*less* when danger loomed in such a way. Thankfully, it seems, we still retain a vestige of that God-given, built-in instinct to reject what threatens our humanness and to do it vehemently.

To be indifferent in face of suffering would itself be a sin. As Oswald Chambers urged: 'Watch the things you shrug your shoulders over.'

But our focus here is not on a possible positive use of anger; nor on what some people – too easily – call 'righteous anger' – a level of indignation that would be best left to Jesus and the saints to feel. Our focus is on the *negative* dimension of anger that we experience all too often. Anger in this sense is both sinful and deadly. It flares up as an ugly, dark energy when our space is invaded, or our supposed comfort-zones are infringed. I am furious at being cut up on the motorway or beaten to the getaway at the traffic lights: I succumb to so-called 'road-rage'. Queuing is a breeding ground for this: I am livid at being jumped at the supermarket checkout and suffer the temporary insanity of 'trolley-rage'. I am typing determinedly away when I unwittingly lean on the keyboard; my computer screen goes berserk and so do I. I want to throw the infuriating machine out of my study window. These are relatively trivial and temporary, though irritating, reminders that, in Christopher Lasch's words, 'rebellion against God is the natural reaction to the discovery that the world was not made for my personal convenience!'[4]

But sadly, sometimes, the bullying and mockery intensify until resentment boils over into violence. So, derided as a 'freak and a loser', Charles Williams, an enraged 15-year-old, takes his father's guns to Santana High School near San Diego, California, on Monday 5 March 2001 and exacts revenge by shooting dead two of his classmates and wounding 13 others.

Positive use of anger is rare but needful: it feeds a legitimate desire for justice. Sinful anger is all too common and fuels a ruthless quest for vengeance. It is a bittersweet and self-destructive emotion.

As Frederick Buechner sees it:

Of the seven deadly sins, anger is the most fun. To lick our wounds, to smack your lips over grievances long past, to roll over your tongue the prospect of bitter confrontations still to come, to savor to the last toothsome morsel both the pain you are given and the pain you are giving back – in many ways it is a feast for a king. The chief drawback is that what you are wolfing down is yourself. The skeleton at the feast is you.[5]

It was to uncover this that God approached Cain with a kind but penetrating question: *'Why are you angry?'* (Gen. 4:6). God asks what can only be called the ultimate *psychological* question, which probes our emotional state. 'Why are you angry? Why is your face downcast?'

THE SOUL'S TRUE HEALER

Now let's be clear right away that God is not here merely trying to pour oil on troubled emotional waters. He will not heal Cain's wound lightly by making him feel better – or, what is even more inadequate – making him feel better about himself. If Cain had had the courage to answer God's question he might have retorted: 'Why am I angry?!! ... I am angry because I feel devastated and humiliated at the core of my very being. You have no idea what it feels like to have something you have carefully prepared rejected by the one to whom it is offered.'

'Tell me about it,' God might have replied.
Tragically, Cain did not respond.

If he had done so, he might have found, in confessing his deeper feelings, a reason for his anger and so turned from the path of violence into the path of healing. This is surely God's aim in asking the question. In short, God is not the therapist stroking egos, acting in a soothing role, but the soul's true healer in a saving role.

As Ray Anderson says, 'We need to listen to what our emotions are telling us about ourselves.'[6] This is exactly what the Lord is trying to get Cain to do. In questioning Cain, the Lord is encouraging him to confront what his emotions – in this case, anger – are telling him about his deeper drives and desires. Anger is specifically *more an emotion than a feeling*. In many cases – not all – when anger is suppressed it causes us to be depressed. In self-defence, we prefer the deadening ache of depression to the unbearable agony of feeling rejected, worthless and deeply resentful of others. However we react, anger is an emotional response to a perceived attack on our self-esteem.

Cain is suffering from *'rejection-rage'*.

At this point it may be worth noting the tragic split in modern Christianity between head and heart. 'Not head knowledge but heart knowledge' has become almost a

mantra urged on us by popular preachers. This is confus-
ing because it is wrong. Biblically the 'heart' is the all-
encompassing centre of the personality, the seat of our
emotions, thoughts and will. In this holistic biblical view of
our humanity, there is no false separation of thought from
feeling. They are inextricably linked.

*Emotions are feelings that we are aware of and can
reflect on.*

The Bible recognises our states of soul but does not
disconnect them from the rational thoughts and moral
choices that interact with them. 'The heart has its reasons.'
When the element of cognition is joined to feeling then we
have an emotion. And we can never sever emotions from
intentions. Ray Anderson helpfully explains the implications
of this when he says that 'we are not judged for having
emotions but we are held accountable for what is intended
by them'.[7]

In Cain's case, it is easy to empathise with Cain's reaction.
No apparent reason is given why God accepts Abel's
offering and not Cain's, or why God favours Abel over Cain.
Perhaps because Cain offers a token of his rich estate while
Abel, a poorer man, offers the choicest part of his, and sheds
blood in doing so. But biblical commentators have not
come up with a satisfactory answer. This is probably
because it is not the point of the story. At a basic level

what matters is to know that *life is unfair* and unjust and we had better well learn to cope with it and the emotional turmoil it causes.

SAVAGE DOGS

The brothers appear equal in every respect with no hint in the text of Abel's superiority. In fact if anything Cain has claims to superiority. He is the older of the two brothers, the only one whose birth is acclaimed by his mother. His name, however enigmatic – perhaps God-acquired – at least provides more significance than Abel's, the 'nobody'![8] Here then perhaps is the inversion of natural precedence. And Cain hates it, and in the end hates both God and his brother for it. 'Why are you angry?' was God's merciful inquiry meant to alert Cain to the potentially lethal feelings festering beneath the surface.

In Peter de Vries's novel *The Blood of the Lamb*, the main character, Don Wanderhope – echoes of Cain here perhaps – loses his daughter to leukemia and reflects angrily:

> Rage and despair are indeed carried about in the heart, but privately, to be let out on special occasions, like savage dogs for exercise, occasions in solitude when God is cursed, birds stoned from the trees or the pillow hammered in darkness.[9]

Envy and jealousy, resentment and rejection, shame and

humiliation – these are the poisons working in Cain's heart. God's question is intended to 'lance the boil' before it bursts into violence and tragedy. 'Self-recovery begins by seeking emotional health through emotional wisdom. Listening to what our emotions are telling us about our feelings is the beginning of wisdom.'[10]

Cain's fate hangs in the balance. Emotions are feelings you can reflect on. There is no foregone conclusion here. The outcome has yet to be decided.

- First, God offers him gracious reassurance – *'If you do what is right, will you not be accepted?'* In other words, Cain is reassured that his acceptance by God does not depend on the quality of his offering but on his reaction to God's freedom and choice. Nothing is fixed in stone at this stage.
- God then gives him an honest warning – *'but if you do not do what is right, sin is crouching at your door'*. This is a graphic image of sin as a dangerous predator lurking in wait to pounce upon its victim. But note again there is nothing predetermined here.
- God issues Cain with a challenging and empowering choice – *'it desires to have you, but you must master it'*. The encouraging implication is surely that Cain has it within him by trusting God to avert the outbreak of 'rejection-rage' or 'brother-rage'.

Sadly, a knowledge of sin is no defence against the power of sin. Cain's body language says it all. Crestfallen he averts his eyes from God and from his brother and closes his ears to God's entreaties.

Let's take our diagnosis further with another biblical case study: that of Israel's first king, Saul.

'RIVAL-RAGE'

David's military success and popularity with the people cause widespread rejoicing. Women flock from the towns singing and dancing in his praise: 'Saul has slain his thousands, and David his tens of thousands.' The king seems not to be a fan of this kind of country music! 'Saul was very angry' (1 Sam. 18:8).

He has been upstaged in the body count. He is not receiving the honour and acclaim due to him as king. Saul can't stand not being 'hero number one'. It might have made a difference if Saul could have viewed David not as merely *greedy* for the throne but as divinely *destined* for the throne. Saul is blinded by an acute attack of *'rival-rage'*. In Cornelius Plantinga's words: 'In the classic case of a star eclipsed by a superstar, Saul sees, fears, and murderously resents the changing of the guard.'[11] He is consumed with jealousy because he is not receiving the credit and applause he believes he has a right to. Jealously produces fear, and fear gives rise to hatred and a desire with murderous intent. Just like Cain in fact. We need a 'heart transplant', a new sense of the sovereignty of God, a new willingness to accept that where man proposes, God disposes; we need a newfound courage to face another's anger and envy without being crushed, a resilient answer that diverts wrath, the turning of the other cheek that confounds the powerful with the meekness that inherits the earth. But for that a gospel and a Saviour will be needed.

The aftermath of an exalted experience or event is often a deep sense of anticlimax. Just then we often feel flat, listless and dispirited. At this point we are vulnerable to attack on our spirits. After the climactic 'high' of Carmel, Elijah is suddenly gripped by fear when he learns that he is on Jezebel's 'most wanted list' (1 Kings 19:1-18). Panic and flight ensue. And when God catches up with him, the prophet is depressed, mired in self-pity, swamped by unworthiness and on the edge of yielding to a death wish! This is a classic description of what is now usually called 'burn-out'. Elijah is spiritually, emotionally and nervously exhausted. At this point God is the Master Counsellor, handling Elijah like fragile china. He prescribes sleep for jaded nerves and an overwrought constitution. He provides a nourishing square meal. God recharges his emotional, nervous and spiritual batteries with a dazzling display of natural effects – earthquake, wind and fire. The pyrotechnics themselves do not induce Elijah out of hiding, but they soften him up, as it were. God then wraps his prophet in a healing silence broken only by a still small whisper of love, which asks: 'What are you doing here?' Once more God's question is meant to elicit information not for God's benefit but for Elijah's!

Depressed people can rarely be talked out of their state of mind. What does often help is a new sense of purpose. This is what happens here. 'Why are you here in this emotional state?' aims at getting Elijah to probe beneath his emotions to rediscover his bedrock reason for living – being a prophet of God. Refreshed and recommissioned, the prophet begins to feel that life is worth living after all.

'REPENTANCE-RAGE'?

Let's take another case: Jonah. Jonah is seized in a fit of what one can only call *'repentance-rage'*!

Let's put God's question, 'Why are you angry?' to the prophet Jonah. Jonah has been commissioned to preach judgment and repentance to the godless city of Nineveh and has promptly run off in the opposite direction (Jonah 4:1-11). Dragged back from disobedience, delivered from the whale, Jonah finally reaches Nineveh to declare the imminent judgment of God on the unrepentant city. Shocked into repentance, the city is spared by God's compassion.

How does Jonah react? Jonah is outraged.

Did Jonah fear for his reputation and that, with Nineveh repenting, he might be thought a false prophet? Possibly, but what seems clear from the text is that he found it so hard to come to terms with God's amazing grace and mercy. 'I knew you were like that, O Lord, I knew you'd do this to me; I feel utterly humiliated; I want to die.'

Have we heard this before? 'Have you any right to be angry?' God asks. 'You're so concerned that your own calm is ruffled, your own self-interest impinged upon. But what about my larger purposes and bigger heart?' When revival came to Nineveh, was Jonah miffed because there was no way he would get the credit?

Then when God grows up a tree to shade the sulking prophet, Jonah fleetingly regains his composure. But when the tree shrivels, Jonah's anger boils over again. Again God's question stops him short. Jonah, *you seem more angry that the plant is lost than that the lost are lost!*

According to Elizabeth Achtemeier, Jonah is being told three things. First, it is being pointed out to him that he has no right at all to say what should happen to Nineveh. Second, God is telling Jonah that he is totally ungrateful for the grace and mercy that has been shown him repeatedly. Third, Jonah is being told – as we are – that God's love extends to the whole, sinful, wicked world of violence and wrong.[12]

The fact is that all sinful anger is deep down a complaint against God. In our natural minds we can't stand 'the sovereign injustice of divine grace'. Grace saves us but humbles and confounds us as well. Grace brings out the worst in us so that it can do the best to us.

This raises the issue of where we derive our deepest satisfaction from. 'Why are you angry? Why are you cast down?' – these are the forms taken by the emotional or psychological question God asks us. To the exiles in Babylon it was put this way: 'Why are you feeling so deeply unsatisfied with life?' (see Isa. 55). You have been sucked into the Babylonian way of doing things. You live life in the fast lane but is it going anywhere? You are working harder and for longer hours, but where is it getting you? Or as the prophet has God ask: 'Why spend money on what is not bread, and your labour on what does not satisfy?'(Isa. 55:1).

Again this is a shrewd plea that we listen to our emotions, to hear what the persistent sense of frustration and unfulfilment is telling us. This nagging feeling of being dissatisfied must not be assuaged superficially. If we listen to the question posed by our inner dissatisfaction, we may detect signs of spiritual health. Hunger for more than the junk food on our cultural menu – money, pleasure, possessions, hobbies and so on – is, in fact, a deeper longing for God Himself.

At this point, it would be a great mistake to assume that Christianity is about the denial of passion or the suppression of desire. Quite the reverse. As C.S. Lewis insisted, the problem is not that our desires are too *strong* but too *weak*![13] We aim too low; we misspend our passions on lower satisfactions, we quench our thirst on cheaper beer. In Sam Storms' words, 'The power of temptation is the false promise that sin will make me happier than God can.'[14] 'Delight yourself in the LORD and he will give you the desires of your heart' urges the psalmist (Psa. 37:4). And his exhortation is not a recipe for selfish religion but a recognition of the undeniable fact that God has built into us an irrepressible hunger and thirst for joy and satisfaction, which can be found only in right relationship with Him. We sin when we refuse God's gifts and seek to 'buy' this pleasure on our own terms in the marketplace of consumerism or entertainment or illicit sex. We moderns tend to reduce everything – including sex – and every person to a commodity to be bought and sold. Precisely here we lose the plot. Such joy comes with grace, 'without money and without price'. Such happiness is genuinely priceless. 'There is no greater way to glorify God,' argues Sam Storms, 'than to find in him the happiness that my soul craves.'[15] But even God's people doubt this or succumb to cultural pressure and need the prophetic question.

WHIRLWIND OF DESIRE

What our emotional outbursts 'tell' us then is that our hearts are restless till they find their rest in God, that our psychological thirst is unquenchable apart from drinking at the fountain of living waters.

I have no doubt that in our 'Oprah Winfrey' culture of emotional voyeurism, virtues like self-restraint and meekness and reticence need to make a comeback. But not at the expense of openness and honesty. Not if it means the return of the grimly repressed, uptight, po-faced Christianity that came out of the deep freeze. Nor does this mean the putting of our emotions into neutral gear; there really is no such state. Medieval Christians identified 'accidie' as one of the cardinal sins. Accidie is apathy and indifference. But this is itself a sin against our God-given instinct for wonder, fascination and curiosity. Boredom is a breeding ground of sin. The bored person is almost crying out, 'Stimulate me … seduce me.' Addictive lifestyles are most often lived by those who were once terminally bored.

Jesus sought the least, the last and the lost. These might have appreciated their plight. But He rattled the cages of the complacent equally. Jesus stirred up a whirlwind of desire wherever He went. He had not come to bring a placebo-like peace but a sword of cutting, raw-edged reality. He had not come to dampen down fires of hope but to inflame them.

He warned, 'Do not labour for the food that perishes but for the food that endures to eternal life' (see John 6:27). This was Jesus' way with the woman at the well. As Ray Anderson says,

> He touched the core of this woman's passion, which hitherto, had been indiscriminately poured out in a series of unfulfilling relationships. What others may have seen as promiscuous sexual passion, Jesus diagnosed as an unfulfilled thirst for a love that gave back as much as it took.[16]

Behind God's probing query lies a gracious invitation: 'Come, all you who are thirsty, come to the waters ... Come, buy wine and milk without money and without cost' (Isa. 55:1). Psalm 50 is a psalm for Cain. 'I have no need of a bull from your stall or of goats from your pens ... If I were hungry I would not tell you, for the world is mine, and all that is in it' (Psa. 50: 9,12). Nothing we do can ever make up a lack in God; nothing we fail to do can deprive Him. Neither Cains nor Abels can ever put God in their debt. It is futile to attempt to 'out-give' Him. 'How can I repay the LORD for all his goodness to me?' asks the psalmist in Psalm 116:12. Answer: 'I will lift up the cup of salvation ...' In other words, 'I will drink even more of his generous grace.' Patterns of jealousy and rejection, competitiveness and depression reflect futile attempts to win some kind of acceptance for ourselves from God. But such acceptance with God is not based on what we have to offer to God but on what He sacrifices for us. Cain's failure is an early instruction in this upside-down grace.

ANGRY OLDER MAN

And that brings us to our last case study where 'rejection-rage', 'rival-rage', and 'repentance-rage' all come together in one furious angry man: the older brother in the parable of the 'two sons' (Luke 15).

When the lost son is fêted and fed with the finest in the father's house, the older brother's simmering anger boils over. 'The older brother became angry and refused to go in' (Luke 15:28). No doubt he was showing the classic symptoms: veins in the neck bulging, pulse rate soaring, lips pursed, eyes narrowing. The older brother is tragically lost in the father's house, looking in from the outer darkness of a self-chosen private hell on the light and joy inside.

Let's put the emotional question to the older son and ask him and ourselves: 'Why are you angry?' There is surely much of the older son in all of us: wanting to live up to expectations, trying all our lives to please, to be dutiful and obliging. Yet all the time like him we may be nursing a hidden curiosity for the disobedient life, secretly envying the footloose prodigals their fun, harbouring a grudging resentment at the hand life has dealt us. And when the prodigal returns to be welcomed and lavished with love and forgiveness, it's all too much! Like Cain, like Jonah, the older brother is angry at sheer grace.

His slave mentality is exposed ('All these years I've been slaving for you'), his service is revealed as a self-righteous obedience ('I never disobeyed your orders'). He complains of favouritism ('He got a calf, I didn't even get a goat'), he exaggerates the prodigal's sins ('He went with "prostitutes"' – is this a glimpse into his own sexual fantasies?). What we see is lifelong mistrust, a career ingratitude, a failure to recognise that all life is pure gift ('everything I have is yours').

ENTITLEMENT OR GIFT?

Why do we get so angry? Why 'road-rage' and every other kind of rage? One factor, says Rebecca Manley Pippert, 'in the contemporary epidemic of anger is that we are brought up believing we are *entitled*'.[17] How like Cain in fact. We need a new sense of perspective that life is a gift, not an entitlement. But Pharisaism is too proud to ask or receive. To him it might feel like dying, for the angry older brother to come inside to the light of exposure and acceptance. But then the lost do get found, the dead can come alive, the hearts frozen over with cold anger can melt once more. Jesus invites us to let Him thaw out of us our anger and pride, our fears and envy at the holy fire of God's forgiveness. Sharing the Father's delight over the lost being found, and the dead coming alive again, we find our inner turmoil and mixed motives swallowed up in the exuberant joy of His kingdom. 'I am convinced,' wrote Henri Nouwen, 'that many of my emotional problems would melt as the snow in the sun if I could let the truth of God's non-comparing love permeate my heart.'[18]

God's question then invites us to find emotional wholeness in Christ. The Holy Spirit-empowered life can enable us to feel and express genuine emotions without being overwhelmed by them. Where else can we go for this than to the crucified God? In Peter de Vries's powerful story – quoted earlier – the central character, Don Wanderhope buys an iced cake to take to his sick daughter, whose condition he believes is improving. Noticing the night nurse slipping into an adjacent church, he follows her in, and learns from her that an infection is sweeping through the hospital and that his daughter's life is threatened. He rushes to visit her, only to find her dying. She dies, he notes with bitter irony, at three o'clock in the afternoon. He returns to the church where he has left the cake. In a rage, he hurls the cake at a crucifix hanging above the door.

> It was miracle enough that the pastry should reach its target at all at that height from the sidewalk. The more so that it should land squarely, just beneath the crown of thorns. Then through scalded eyes I seemed to see the hands free themselves of the nails and move slowly towards the soiled face. Very slowly, very deliberately,

with infinite patience, the icing was wiped from the eyes and flung away ... with the kind sobriety of one whose voice could be heard saying: 'Suffer the children to come unto me ... for of such is the kingdom of heaven.'

So, adds De Vries, 'Wanderhope was found at the place which ... was said to be the only alternative to the muzzle of a pistol: the foot of the cross.'[19]

HE THIRSTED FOR US

The Christ of the cross, we dare to believe, absorbs the anger and hate we feel at being overlooked. In His cross He absorbs the rage for violence we feel at being slighted or denied our perceived rights.

He died the innocent victim. He did not revile when He was reviled, but trusted to Him Who judges justly. He forgave His enemies from the cross. He plumbed the depths of God-forsakenness.

He drained to the dregs the cup of wrath our sins had mingled, He thirsted in tongue and heart, in the furthest desert of our emotional emptiness and psychological deprivation. But He declined the cheap wine that might have offered quick-fix alleviation.

He surrendered His divine entitlement for the sake of us

sinners. He forwent His 'diplomatic immunity' from pain and death for our sake. In His wounds is our healing and wholeness.

Peace, joy and self-control flow from the life that has died with Christ. The fruits that flourish in the soil of co-crucifixion are the fruits of His own Spirit. Empowered by the Spirit we can, as James says, slow down and put the brakes on before we let our rage erupt, knowing, as we do, that human anger does not produce the righteousness of God. Do it before nightfall, Paul tells the Ephesians, don't go to bed nursing your anger, but surrender again to healing mercy. Only the Spirit of the crucified Jesus can coax us to open up again in this way when we have been hurt, to love again when we have been rejected.

> Crushed by the tempter, feelings lie buried that grace
>   will restore.
> Touched by a loving hand, wakened by kindness, chords
>   that were broken will vibrate once more.[20]

But whenever we take the risk of handing our life over to Sovereign Love, we receive it again transformed, no longer as an entitlement to be exploited but as a gift of grace to be enjoyed.

Q5

'WHERE IS YOUR BROTHER?'
(Genesis 4:9)

'I HAVE A DREAM THAT ONE DAY ON THE RED HILLS OF Georgia the sons of former slaves and the sons of former slaveowners will be able to sit down together at a table of brotherhood. I have a dream ...'[1]

Martin Luther King's passion and eloquence on Capitol Hill at the end of the march on Washington in August 1963 brought the dream to life. Whatever his many flaws, King was prepared to die to keep the dream alive.

But the dream of brotherhood got off to a nightmare start. The rage that batters against its blocked goals turns murderous. Cain kills Abel.

So the Lord comes asking questions. *'Where is your brother?'* Just as God had asked Adam, 'Where are you?' he now asks Cain, 'Where is your brother?' If the first was the great *theological* question, the latter constitutes the great *social* question. God is concerned not only with what we have done with *Him* but what we have done with our *brother*. The two issues are inextricably linked.

We cannot love God without loving our neighbour. God puts this question to Cain not at an altar or sanctuary but out in the fields, stopping him in his tracks in the midst of his working life. In other words, this question prevents us taking refuge in a safety zone called 'individual religion' or 'personal devotion'. There is no realm of God we can

113

inhabit that is insulated from the concerns of brother, spouse, neighbour, friend, colleague or indeed fellow-human being. We simply cannot have a relationship with God that does not at the same time include our relationships with other people. The Bible knows nothing of a spiritual salvation divorced from a concern for social justice. So while people may protest that they have never heard a direct address from God about their relationship with Him, few if any have not in one way or another heard the question: 'Where is your brother?' This will hopefully not be a reference to the person you killed, but to the person you gossiped about unkindly, ignored, slighted, patronised, disregarded or generally passed by on the other side of!

As a young boy, the late Rabbi Hugo Gryn survived Auschwitz. He entered the camp on a bright, sunny day with vapour trails high in the clear sky. He felt sure God would miraculously intervene to save him. Assigned to the wood-cutting yard, he tried to remember on Yom Kippur as many of the set prayers as he could. He broke down into prolonged sobbing until, he recalls, he lapsed into curious peace and sensed that God too was crying. 'I would like you understand,' he writes,

> that in that builder's yard on the Day of Atonement, I found God. But not the God I had childishly clung to until those jet streams dissolved over Auschwitz. People

sometimes ask me: 'Where was God in Auschwitz?' I believe that God was there himself – violated and blasphemed. The real question is: 'Where was *man* in Auschwitz?'[2]

'BEING-WITH'

We are, of course, inescapably social beings. It was 'not good for man to be alone', according to Genesis 2:18. Created in God's image, we are called to reflect that image by living as 'male and female'. This refers, of course, primarily, to the God-blessed union between man and woman. But undoubtedly it also makes the larger point that within the God-given joy of being unique individuals we can only know what it is to be a truly human being in relation with others.

Since the work of Martin Buber and Karl Barth, modern theologians have fruitfully explored the *relational* dimension of our creation 'in the image of God'. Our essential 'being' is a *'being-with'* so that by definition the human being is a being-in-relationship. Douglas John Hall spells this out as follows.

Authentic humanness means:

- being-with   – coexistence
- being-for   – pro-existence
- being-together – communion, community, covenant

Inauthentic or 'fallen' humanity means:

- being-alone   – autonomy, selfish independence
- being-against – estrangement and alienation
- being-above – pride, attempt at mastery
- being-below – sloth, escape from responsibility.[3]

So it is our relationships that help to make us who we are. David Ford speaks of the 'community of the heart'[4] made up of all the voices and faces we have given a home to. Many of these are permanent and welcome residents, giving warmth and nourishment when we think of them. Other voices and faces are less comfortable, bringing a challenge to our conscience or a sting to the memory. As we noted earlier, inside our hearts live the faces and voices that built us up and energised us by believing in us; but alongside them are the others whose memory shrinks us, those who put us down and from whom we learnt 'the slow rustings of shame'. But we are who we are because of these faces and voices; they are woven into the texture of our identity. Only a select few are invited in and asked to stay.

We lack the capacity to be on intimate terms with many. Yet we are called every day to offer what David Ford calls the 'hospitality of the heart' to a wider circle of strangers, clients, customers, neighbours and service workers of every kind. And here we may be surprised by grace. For when Jesus is central to the core of our being, when He is the

Chief Guest – or better, as we live 'before His face' as Lord – He enlarges our capacity for heart-hospitality. By His overwhelming love, we can extend our boundaries to give a touch and taste of Jesus to poor and needy, to postmen (mine's called Mike) and milk-delivery men (mine's called Jon) and passers-by!

BROTHERS-IN-LAW AND VEGETABLES

Yet as we may all ruefully acknowledge, being a social being brings headaches as well as joys. When Cain is asked, 'Where is your brother?' it threatens to expose his deep-seated jealousy of Abel and resentment against God. 'If only I had been born to some other parent, or married someone else!' And so it goes on with, no doubt, very good reason in many cases.

Cain, put on the spot and in cynical mood, responds with a query of his own: 'Am I my brother's keeper?' It is a defiant but, in Eugene Peterson's words, a 'flip and lonely question'[5] that already shows how alienated he is from real community. Cain's reply is an attempt to pass the whole thing off as a joke: 'Am I my keeper's keeper?' To which of course the strict answer is 'No'. None of us is ever intended to be in that sense anyone else's 'keeper'. Only zoos and prisons have 'keepers'! We are not meant to 'manage' other people in this way. No, we are not each other's 'keepers'. Martin Luther King insisted that he wanted to be the white man's brother, not his brother-in-law!

How we see each other is crucial. One of the most moving books I have read is Christopher de Vinck's *The Power of the Powerless: A Brother's Legacy of Love*, which tells the story of his severely handicapped brother, Oliver.

> I grew up in the house where my brother was on his back for thirty-two years, in the same corner of his room, under the same windows, beside the same yellow walls. He was blind, mute, his legs were twisted. He didn't have the strength to lift his head or the intelligence to learn anything. Oliver was born with severe brain damage which left him and his body in a permanent state of helplessness.

De Vinck goes on to describe how his parents cared for their son until his death, and how, as a schoolteacher, he began to tell his brother's story to his class. 'One day,' he writes,

> I was trying to describe Oliver's lack of response, how he had been spoon-fed every morsel he ever ate, how he never spoke. A boy in the last row, raised his hand and said, 'Oh, Mr. de Vinck. You mean he was a vegetable.'

Instantly recalling how his family had fed Oliver, tickled his chest to make him laugh, lowered the shades at the window to protect his sensitive skin from the sun, Christopher de

Vinck stammered his reply. 'Well, I guess you would call him a vegetable. I called him Oliver, my brother. You would have loved him.'[6]

THE JACOB SYNDROME
God's question then clearly implies we are responsible for knowing where our brother is; we are responsible for our relationships in so far as we can influence them.

Israel's own story had problematic origins, fraught with fraternal rivalries, victims and victimisers. Take the prime victimiser. The patriarchal narrative tells honestly about the long-running feud between Jacob and Esau. Jacob is a scheming, two-faced liar, the kind of man from whom you would not have bought a second-hand camel, the son who tricked his own brother out of his legal birthright. And yet, this is the man who is made father of the nation, the black sheep of the patriarchal family turned by grace into the princely shepherd of God's people! This is what grace can do even in a dysfunctional family.

And then there is Joseph, the victim of fraternal jealousy and cruelty. Not that I don't feel a tinge of sympathy for Joseph's brothers. He must have seemed a bit of a 'spoiled brat' and a pain in the neck with his high-flown ideas and ego-centred dreams! He certainly suffered for it in the end. Thrown into a pit and sold into slavery in Egypt. This was indeed a strange and paradoxical way for Abraham's descendants to enter Egypt. But God was with Joseph in protecting him and redeeming his life from futility so that Joseph emerges as prime minister of Egypt, in a position to bless or harm his erstwhile antagonistic brothers. The scene when Joseph reveals his true identity to them is one of the most moving in the Old Testament. Looking back on the painful family saga, Joseph is nevertheless able to discern the providential hand of God: 'You intended to harm me, but God intended it for good to accomplish ... the saving of many lives' (Gen. 50:20). If nothing else the patriarchal stories reassure us that God can bring blessing out of the worst family situation.

It is, therefore, not surprising that Israel's first obligation was to love God and one's neighbour. No wonder that, enshrined in the covenant law, was the need to care for the widows and orphans, strangers and immigrants. Mrs Thatcher may have been misquoted when, as UK Prime Minister, she is alleged to have said: 'There is no such thing as society.' But the remark sums up only too well the working creed of many people in our fast-track, individualistic world. 'This life is no rehearsal, grab what you can'; 'What's it got to do with me?' 'Look out for number one, that's what I say.'

It was not so in the beginning, even in Israel. Mindful of the oppressive and unjust social system she had endured under Pharaoh, Israel was entrusted with a law that aimed to create precisely that just, free and neighbourly society which Israel had been denied in slavery. Among a people who had once been slaves in a foreign country, aliens and slaves were to be treated with special respect. Neighbours were to be loved and respected. Family relationships were sacrosanct. Human life was precious. When God's people forgot this calling, the prophets forcefully reminded them. Amos inveighed against commercial malpractice; exposing as phonies those religious business types who 'sold the needy for a pair of shoes', and who were impatient for Sabbath to end so that they could get back to their corrupt, exploitative and lucrative trade. Amos sent the haunting question, 'Where is you brother?' reverberating round every bank, business and farm in Israel!

PEOPLE HUSBANDRY

The essayist, Wendell Berry – by turns academic, farmer, and conservationist – is one of the USA's most perceptive social critics. He links the modern despoiling of the environment with the misuse of people. In the mind of the so-called 'boomer' generation, he argues, people become expendable if treated only on the basis of crude economic metaphor.

Any person or thing is understood as a mine having a 'limited yield'; when the yield falls below expectation, it is time to move on. It is easy to see that the boomer's mind must be equally destructive of nature and of humanity – hard on landscape and on spouses, hard on children and on other small creatures.[7]

To exercise dominion is our creative calling, whether over the natural world or over ourselves. Sin corrupts our royal vocation. Abortion, for example, apart from the likely death of the mother, is now widely defended solely on the basis of 'a woman's right to exercise control over her own body'. But, as Berry points out,

> The usual qualification had it that if you can control your own body only by destroying another person's body, then control has come much too late. Self-mastery is the appropriate way to control one's own body, not surgery.[8]

Jesus ups the stakes of social consciousness by saying that anyone who is angry with their brother is liable to judgment just as a murderer is (Matt. 5:21-22).

Jesus causes an even greater stir by radically redefining family bonds. In the presence of His own natural family He shocks His hearers by declaring: 'Whoever does God's will is my brother and sister and mother' (Mark 3:35). He is the Messianic Lord at the centre of this newfound family. So closely is He identified with its members and they with Him that what is done to Him can be said to be done to them and vice-versa. 'He who receives you receives me, and he who receives me receives the one who sent me' (Matt. 10:40). Our experience of God depends it seems not only on how well we receive Jesus but also on how well we welcome each other!

In one of His last parables, the story of the sheep and the goats, one awesome criterion of judgment is the way we have treated the messengers of Jesus, those He calls His 'brothers'. In so far as we minister to the needs of His agents – visiting them when imprisoned for the gospel, feeding them when hungry, sheltering them when a stranger to us – we are ministering to Jesus Himself (Matt. 25:31–46)! What does this say to us about our solidarity with the suffering and persecuted Christians into today's world?

Just such a realisation was central to the call and conversion of Saul of Tarsus. He discovered to his horror that in hurting Christians he was hurting the Messiah! Perhaps this was what sparked him later to write of the Church as so closely bound up with Jesus as to be His very body! Certainly in the body of Christ we have ample opportunity to express our need of and dependence on one another. There where Jesus is head, let brotherly love continue! Each of us has our own story and must give our own answer to God for how we play our part (John 21:22; Rom. 14:12). In writing to the Galatians, Paul carefully balances individual freedom and obligation to others. Each of us has our own distinctive load to carry (Gal. 6:5). The word he uses (*phortion*) suggests the pack assigned to a soldier. I must carry my pack; no one else can carry it for me. But, says Paul in the same context, we are called to 'carry one another's burdens' (*baros* in Greek) for in this way we 'fulfil the law of Christ' (v. 2). Properly attending to our own loads and being willing to bear each other's undue burdens frees us, Paul argues, from competitiveness and stops us comparing ourselves with each other in damaging ways (vv. 3-4).

THIS SON OF YOURS

Consider with me one last time the attitude of the older brother in the parable Jesus told of the father with two sons. He was bitterly angry, you recall, at the father's lavish welcome for the homecoming prodigal. So angry is he, in fact, that he distances himself from the family altogether. Note how he addresses his 'father' disrespectfully as 'you' and refers to the prodigal not as 'my brother' but as 'this son of yours'! Yet he is in no position to act like this. He is as servile in his relationship with the father as the younger son had been. He is 'outside' of the house too, and yet the father goes outside to plead with him as he had run out to meet the prodigal. Grace will not let us climb on our high horse and disown a younger generation of returning prodigals. Jimmy Long, who was quoted earlier, notes in his close study of Generation X how most young people come from broken homes and yet long for real community. He points out that in the 1950s and 1960s many popular TV shoes were built around a traditional family. No longer. Soap operas now features adultery, cohabitation and divorce as a matter of course, along with teenage sex and pregnancies, and even

124

incest. If the media are to be believed, there are no normal, happy families anywhere. This both mirrors society's mess and no doubt reinforces it. We are drip-fed daily the idea that this sad caricature of relationships is normal! But it's not: this is not the way it was supposed to be. Underneath, many people sense it and long to belong.

Significantly the most popular TV show of the late 1990s was *Friends* – where a bunch of rather footloose and self-absorbed '30-somethings' do nevertheless 'look out for each other', as the jargon goes. This tide of longing for relationships laps at our door. As T.S. Eliot said:

> The desert is not remote in southern tropics,
> the desert is not only round the corner,
> the desert is squeezed in the tube-train next to you,
> the desert is in the heart of your brother.[9]

VORTEX OF LOVE

Such relationships are possible because in Christ we have been re-enfolded in the Trinity love and life of God. In Christ we are loved with the same love with which the Father loves the Son. The ultimate reality in the universe is relational. God is love.

In Jesus Christ we are drawn into the vortex of love[10] within the Godhead. We are empowered by such a relationship of love to love in return. We can love as we are loved. The love of Father and Son, which embraces us and holds us together in community, demonstrates who we are to the world. The image of God as loving relationship is once more by redemption made visible and tangible in the world. Paul argues strongly with the Galatians that it's grace not race that counts. Through the faithfulness of Jesus, God is finally achieving the one covenant family He has set His heart on. No longer are the settled divisions of the world of any significance: now 'you are all sons of God through faith in Christ Jesus ... there is neither Jew nor Greek, slave nor free, male nor female, for you are all one in Christ Jesus' (Gal. 3:26,28). Tribal antipathies, cultural class barriers, domestic strife dissolve in Christ. Foreigner or friend, married or unmarried, all can find salvation in Christ and become part of the one people of God. Now that has to be the best news there is for a strife-torn world, whether in Northern Ireland, Serbia, Africa, the Middle East or your home and mine.

THE FAMILY TREE

At crisis times we want our family and friends round us. How comforted Jesus must have been in the agony on the cross to see His mother and closest associate standing there. Typically He's thinking more of them than Himself and comforts them with amazing and creative words. Speaking to His mother, He says: 'Dear woman, here is your son', and to the disciple, 'Here is your mother' (John 19:26,27).

Just here, on the level ground at the foot of the cross, the Church was born. Consider the words of Richard Bauckham and Trevor Hart:

> Just as Jesus' mother and the Beloved Disciple would not otherwise have been related, had not Jesus at his death brought them together, and charged them with being mother and son to each other, so the church is the community of people who would not otherwise be related but whom the crucified Jesus brings together, forging new relationships through his death for us.[11]

This is both joy and obligation. As Ronald Wallace points out:

> If Mary turned away from the cross that day with some of her burden lifted, John turned away from it with a new and heavy responsibility thrust into his personal home life.[12]

So for us the Church is no abstraction but flesh and blood relations, characterised by family affection, brotherly love and bonds of trusting friendship. What other incentive do we need than the cross to seek the unity of all Christians? Our fellowship is formed by the one broken body, which does not need to be torn apart again by our fractiousness and divisions. Let's return to the level ground beneath the cross,

127

so to drink of the one fountain of love that the world may know we are His disciples by our love for one another.

> It is the cross that binds John to Mary, and binds all disciples to one another in a mutual gift of self. Christ is the gift and Christ enables us to give the gift, which is finally the gift of Christ.[13]

The Holy Spirit, Who is the Spirit of unity and fellowship, will see to that, if we let Him. As John Taylor put it in his classic study of the work of the Holy Spirit, 'Not in our greater goodness, then, but in our openness to one another in Christ's name, the Spirit possesses us. But,' he went on,

> the Spirit does not give himself where our encounters are glib, masked exchanges of second-hand thoughts. Our defences must be down, broken entirely by intense joy or by despair. One way or the other we must come to the end of ourselves.[14]

So the apostle John warns us not to 'be like Cain' who 'belonged to the evil one and murdered his brother'. In fact, 'Anyone who hates his brother is a murderer.' This how we know what love is: 'Jesus Christ laid down his life for us. And we ought to lay down our lives for our brothers' (1 John 3:12–16). This is costly, tough love. It means a laying-down of sophistication and self-righteousness, a laying-down of my life as a carpet of honour for others to walk on.

It means a resilient willingness to be vulnerable again. But what a sense of enormous relief it is when we recognise in some people a heart that has achieved a 'second naiveté' – someone who has been through it all, who has loved and perhaps lost, or at least has been let badly down, who has perhaps been abused or taken advantage of but who, in a childlike trust rooted in God's love, is ready to risk extending once again the welcome and 'hospitality of their hearts'. This too is a miracle that grace can achieve.

BETTER THINGS

Abel's death was no 'perfect murder'. Cain did not get away with it. He is condemned to a wandering life. The perpetrator's fate is 'to lose all sense of belonging, and identification with a community. It is to become rootless and detached.'[15] As for the victim, the cry of his innocent blood went up from the very ground stained by it and was heard by God. But the blood shed by God's Son at Calvary speaks 'a better word than the blood of Abel' (Heb. 12:24). Its message is not revenge but reconciliation. In William Lane's words, 'It "speaks" in the idiom of grace rather than vengeance.'[16] As Philip Hughes vividly sees it,

> this horrifying violence of fratricide in which, impelled by hatred, brother sheds the blood of brother, and which displays the depravity and enormity of sin and its consequences for society, is offset and nullified by the terrible violence of Christ's death in which, impelled by

sheer love, he of his own will sheds his blood for us whom he is not ashamed to call his brothers.[17]

And Oxford theologian Oliver O'Donovan comments on the 'better word' spoken by the sprinkled blood of Jesus:

> It puts to rest the cry of outraged innocence which Cain's civilisation could never silence. Abel was not vindicated, but Jesus was; and by his vindication put an end to the unfinished business of nature's justice. But where Abel's vindication would have meant the destruction of Cain's race, Jesus' vindication meant a new beginning for it.

So, concludes O'Donovan, 'he took the place of the hanged man, he took the place of his executioners, under condemnation ... He represented both innocent Abel and guilty Cain, and reconciled them to each other and to God.'[18]

We little realise, in our obsessively therapeutic climate, that sin is not only spiritual sickness but lines us up as implacable enemies of God. This 'enmity' towards God – which Paul speaks of – makes us the object of wrath and judgment unless God Himself interposes His Son to spare and save us. And this is amazingly exactly what He has done. The blood of this innocent victim, nailed up between two political terrorists though He was not one, speaks volumes; it speaks salvation to us all.

And the alienation and estrangement from our own true selves, from others and from God, that is the source of so much emotional anguish and torment, is met and matched at the cross. The spiral of violence that spawns intertribal, racial, ethnic and domestic violence is broken at the cross. The mark of Cain protected him even in his restless wanderings. But the cross of Christ is the door to the father's house for all Cains, prodigals and older brothers. Whatever else heaven is, it is home! And home, if the parable is anything to go by, is final feasting, festivity and hugely joyful celebration; a party that goes on forever!

Jesus died to keep the dream alive; He rose again to make it possible.

He left us a legacy of brotherly love, which we can only gratefully and obediently cash in.

RSVP

How might we respond to God's tough and tender inquiries?

COME HOME

God asks the basic *theological* question, 'Where are you?' – 'Where are you in your relationship with Me'? – because He wants us to *'come home'*. We can answer God by dropping our self-defences, discarding our disguises, emerging from our hideouts, and being reconciled to Him through the death of His Son and so reinstated in the life He appoints for us.

PRAYERFUL RESPONSE

Father, I have lost my place in Your scheme of things and lost my bearings in mine. I want to come home, and to come home all the way to Your holy and happy heart. Just as I am, without one plea but that Your Son has died for me, I come. I surrender to Your arms of love opened to embrace me on the cross. Make me not what I deserve to be but all that You created me to be. In Jesus' name, Amen.

PERSONAL RESPONSE

_____

_____

_____

COME TO OUR SENSES

With the second question, the *ideological* question, 'Who told you?' we are urged to *come to our senses*. So we answer God by recognising how prone we are to self-deception, by switching off all other beguiling voices and by retuning to the word of truth. We make the initial drastic about-face, a radical change of mental and moral direction in order to embrace the kingdom of God. We embark on an on-going repentance, which is the renewal of our minds that reprograms us with truth.

PRAYERFUL RESPONSE

Father, help me to pick out Your voice in the cacophony of noise that engulfs me. Give me ears to hear the truth of the gospel of Jesus Christ. I shut my mouth and fall silent before You, all excuses exhausted and all arguments at an end. Send Your Spirit to renew my mind for courageous non-conformity to worldly values and for the risky doing of Your will. For the sake of the kingdom, Amen.

PERSONAL RESPONSE

_____

_____

_____

_____

GOD'S QUESTIONS

_____
_____
_____
_____
_____
_____
_____
_____
_____
_____
_____
_____
_____
_____
_____
_____
_____
_____
_____
_____
_____
_____
_____
_____
_____

COME CLEAN

We 'own our own stories' by honestly facing the *moral and ethical* question, which asks 'What have you done?' By admitting our guilt and confessing known sins we *come clean* and accept that we are accountable not to ourselves or society, but essentially to God. Receiving 'forgiveness through his blood' by faith, redeemed from guilt and judgment, we are freed to reassume the right level of responsibility for our actions and attitudes.

PRAYERFUL RESPONSE

Father, I have sinned against heaven and in Your sight. I dare to 'own my own story' and confess, 'I did that, I said that, that was me.' By virtue of the blood Your Son shed, forgive me my sins, cleanse and accept me. Redeem all the potential You invested in me and by Your Spirit make me eager, as a grateful forgiven-forgiver, to do good works. Through Jesus Christ our Lord, Amen.

PERSONAL RESPONSE

_____

_____

_____

_____

_____

_____

GOD'S QUESTIONS

_____

_____

_____

_____

_____

_____

_____

_____

_____

_____

_____

_____

_____

_____

_____

_____

_____

_____

_____

_____

_____

COME OPEN

The *psychological* question, 'Why are you angry?' is an invitation to *come open*, to listen to our emotions not in a preoccupied and obsessive way but in order to hear what they are telling us about our deeper intentions and goals. As we release our feelings, we gain a truer self-knowledge and self-acceptance in the love of God, and find ourselves on the road to restored emotional integrity as the Spirit brings forth the fruits of lives co-crucified with Christ.

PRAYERFUL RESPONSE

Father, I take the risk of expressing to You my most powerful feelings, knowing that Your great shock-absorbing heart will not flinch from even my deepest pain or rage. I thank You that Jesus plumbed the depths of forsakenness and thirst for me on the cross. By His wounds heal my wounded soul and purify the deep springs of my heart. By Your Spirit, release from deep within me a flow of passionate praise and fervent love, with the joy and laughter, tears and grief, of someone on the Jesus way to being truly human again. For Your glory, Amen.

PERSONAL RESPONSE

_____

_____

_____

COME TOGETHER

In answering the fifth and final question, the *social and relational* question, 'Where is your brother?' we are moved to *come together*. By grace through faith in the crucified and risen Jesus we are being recreated for true community as part of the one covenant family of God. Drawn into the Trinity life and love of God, embraced with the same love with which the Father loved the Son, we are learning to speak truthfully and lovingly to each other, relearning in fact the skills of being human once more.

'To be a responsible person is to find one's own role and then, funded by the grace of God, to fill this role and to delight in it.'[1]

PRAYERFUL RESPONSE

Father, I recognise with awe that You have made me a unique individual. Release me from being arrogantly independent or of allowing myself to be crushingly over-dependent on others. I acknowledge that I have been redeemed for healthy relationships. Immersed, as I am, by faith and baptism in Your Trinity of love, I know You love me with the same love with which You love the Son in the Spirit. By Your same Spirit make me so free in Your holy love that I may be able to rejoice with all returning prodigals in the festival of freedom and homecoming. Amen.

PERSONAL RESPONSE

_____

_____

_____

_____

_____

_____

_____

_____

_____

_____

_____

_____

_____

_____

_____

_____

_____

_____

_____

_____

_____

_____

_____

POSTSCRIPT

God's questions represent the most urgent invitations we can ever receive. They override all other requests. Nothing is more important than that we respond to them sooner rather than later, and just as we are, whether in weakness in strength. Responding to them means recognising the *fact of sin* and the *reality of salvation*.

In the first place, each of the Lord's questions exposes an aspect of our 'fallenness'. To be described as 'fallen' is to receive a backhanded tribute to our moral grandeur and spiritual dignity. The language seems appropriate enough. We have fallen *from* a great height ('a little lower than the angels'), fallen *off* a high throne ('let them have dominion'), and fallen *short* of our lofty and noble calling ('the glory of God').

Recently some Christian theologians have objected to the term 'the Fall' as an imposition on the text of Genesis rather than an exposition of it; at once too Pauline, too Augustinian and too demeaning! The odd theologian, like Matthew Fox, seems to deny the reality of sin altogether. Very odd indeed! Even more bizarrely, quasi-Gnostic thinkers, both ancient and modern, seek to construe the Genesis story not as falling *down* but as a Fall *upwards*, initiating humankind into an intended enlightenment!

No. The language of 'Fall' still rings true to me as a way of summarising what's not right about the human condition. G.K. Chesterton somewhere says something to the effect that there are many angles at which we can *fall over* but only one at which we can stay upright!

We know this on every hand. For individuals, families, and nations, things *fall apart* as in Yeats' oft-quoted lines:

> Things fall apart; the centre cannot hold;
> Mere anarchy is loosed upon the world.[1]

Mental breakdown, marriage failure, war – symptoms of a dysfunctional world that has *fallen away* from grace, surrendering to centrifugal forces tearing it away from the heart of the Creator. The One Holy Will in which everything coheres and co-operates is splintered into a myriad competing wills.

So we *fall into* debt as we fall into sin; and we *fall behind* with the repayments, incurring a deficit no legalism can make good. We *fall out* with God and with each other, making enemies of friends, stereotyping strangers rather than entertaining angels unawares. And the *'fall out'* from these 'nuclear explosions' settles its poisonous dust on the psychiatrist's couch, the divorce court and the battlefield. Our best laid plans for progress *fall through* the thin ice of our self-confident modernity, or we *fall ill* with a terminal disease, which crushes the soul with heavy loathing.

Yes: *'fallenness'* seems an altogether appropriate term.

But, thankfully, each of the Lord's questions reveals an aspect of His saving intentions and activity on our behalf.

However original sin is, grace is more original still!

However stark the reality of our sin, so much the more radiant is the reality of our salvation through Jesus Christ.

> If death got the upper hand through one man's wrongdoing, can you imagine the breathtaking recovery life makes, sovereign life, in those who grasp with both hands this wildly extravagant life-gift, this grand setting-everything-right, that this one man Jesus Christ provides?
>
> Romans 5:21, *The Message*

THE REAL WORLD OF SALVATION

Jesus Christ is the real exception to the rule of sin and death. He does things differently. He never 'falls'; he *comes down*.

He is the great 'Yes' among the grudging ranks of 'naysayers'. He comes as part of the divine conspiracy to inflict mercy. He has no greatness thrust upon Him but stoops to conquer.

Unashamed to call us His brothers and sisters, He strikes out fiercely into the forbidding desolation of our far country.

As the true Light, He pursues us relentlessly down the dark escape routes of our moral and intellectual confusion.

He outdoes the older son in His zeal for the Father's house. He outruns the prodigal in the profligacy of His self-giving.

He enacts the Father's welcome by His outstretched arms on the cross.

He has a rendezvous with death and meets it. The tenacious holiness of love collides with the tawdry heinousness of sin at the crossroads of history.

The death we deserved is the death we are given – the death of God the Son. Buried in the black hole of our shame and forsakenness, God raises Him up.

He achieves the great reversal, passing against the grain from death to life.

His uprising is a successful revolt against the tyranny of death.

He achieves a real atonement, endorsed by real resurrection, which means real salvation, solid joys and lasting treasure.

But, for us, wrote John Oman, 'it means going back to God all the way, to God as He is, not as, before we came to ourselves, we should wish Him to be.' The only condition is that we abandon pretence and face the reality of sin and of salvation.

> The absence of guile, the absence of all desire to shield oneself in any way from falsehood or derive profit from anything save sincerity and truth, is here at once the condition and the consequence of forgiveness.[2]

So as Mark Buchanan assures us,

> Every day God offers us the real thing – His holiness. Real holiness is truth in the inner parts, God's wisdom spoken in the inmost place. Real holiness is being naked and not being ashamed. Real holiness is coming into the light. Real holiness is telling ourselves the truth, no matter what. Real holiness is calling sin by its real name.[3]

ETERNAL EASTER LAUGHTER

Because of Easter, our tragic, comic, heroic human story is not bound to end only in tears. There was, suggested G.K.

147

Chesterton in the final sentences of *Orthodoxy*, one thing that was 'too great for God to show us when he walked upon our earth; and I have sometimes fancied that it was his mirth'.[4]

> Laughter is praise of God because it is a gentle echo of God's laughter, of the laughter that pronounces judgment on all history. Laughter is praise of God because it foretells the eternal praise of God at the end of time, when those who must weep here on earth will laugh.[5]

Like Sarah and Abraham before us, we are slow to catch on to the Isaac-type humour of a God Who gives life to the dead and calls into existence the things that do not exist. When, finally, we get the joke of resurrection sprung on us, then we may well 'fall' again – only this time it will be to 'fall about' laughing at the absurdity of grace before we fall flat on our faces, stunned by the sheer wonder of it all.

THE WAY THINGS ARE

God's questions make us accountable to Him, forcing us to confront the real-life issues of sin and salvation. The pay-off of sin is deathly misery; the gift of God's salvation is eternal laughter.

According to the Bible, this is simply how it is, always, in every place.

Wherever I go I carry with me the words of Corrie ten Boom reflecting on life in Ravensbruck Concentration Camp. 'Sometimes,' she recalls,

> I would slip the Bible from its little sack with hands that shook, so mysterious had it become to me. It was new; it had just been written. I marveled sometimes that the ink was dry. I had believed the Bible always, but reading it now had nothing to do with belief. *It was simply a description of the way things were* - of hell and heaven, of how men act and how God acts.[6]

What a telling phrase - 'simply a description of the way things were' - the way things are. It is to this reality we are laid bare and have to answer.

God's questions are as

> sharp as a surgeon's scalpel, cutting through everything, whether doubt or defense, laying us open to listen and obey. Nothing and no one is impervious to God's Word. We can't get away from it - no matter what.
>
> Hebrews 4:12-13, *The Message*

At the last, our best hope lies in trusting that the One Who diagnoses our condition is the Healer of it; that the One Who asks the probing questions is Himself the Answer.

NOTES

PREFACE

1. Abraham Heschel, *'Who Is Man?'* (Stanford: Stanford University Press, 1965), p.74.
2. Earl F. Palmer, *The Book that James Wrote* (Grand Rapids: Eerdmans, 1997), p.xii.
3. Frederick Buechner, *Wishful Thinking* (London: Mowbray, 1993), p.93.
4. Quoted by Douglas D. Webster, *Selling Jesus* (Downers Grove: IVP, 1992), p.24.
5. Daniel Taylor, *The Myth of Certainty* (Waco: Word, 1986), p.94.
6. Lewis B. Smedes, *Shame and Grace: Healing the Shame We Don't Deserve* (San Francisco: HarperCollins, 1993), p.159.

INVITATION

1. For intriguing use of Charles Shultz's *Peanuts* cartoon strip in the interest of theology, see Robert Short, *The Gospel According to Peanuts* (Glasgow: Collins Fontana, 1968), and *The Parables of Peanuts* (Glasgow: Collins Fontana, 1969).
2. P.T. Forsyth, *The Justification of God* (London: Independent Press, 1917, reprinted 1948), pp.215–216.
3. Daniel Migliore, *Faith Seeking Understanding* (Grand Rapids: Eerdmans, 1991), p.5.

4. One thinks for a start of the lament psalms, the book of Job, Jesus' cry of dereliction from the cross, Paul's dialogue without God about his unremoved 'thorn in the flesh', and the martyrs' 'How long, Lord?' in the Apocalypse.

5. Henri Nouwen, *In the House of the Lord* (London: Darton, Longman & Todd, 1985), p.5.

6. Migliore, *Faith Seeking Understanding*, p.5.

7. Nouwen, *In the House of the Lord*, p.4.

8. Ibid, p.5.

9. Abraham Heschel, *God in Search of Man* (New York: Noonday Press, 1990), p.137.

10. Nouwen, *In the House of the Lord*, p.5.

11. Michael Horton, *Beyond Culture Wars* (Chicago: Moody Press, 1994), p.188.

12. Donald G. Bloesch, *A Theology of Word and Spirit: Christian Foundations*, vol. 1 (Downers Grove: IVP, 1992), p.128.

13. Eugene H. Peterson, *Five Smooth Stones for Pastoral Work* (Atlanta: John Knox Press, 1980), p.140.

14. Bloesch, *A Theology of Word and Spirit*, p.230.

15. Philip D. Kenneson and James L. Street, *Selling out the Church: The Dangers of Church Marketing* (Nashville: Abingdon, 1997), p.157.

16. Anthony J. Gittens, *A Presence that Disturbs: A Call to Radical Discipleship* (London: St Pauls, 2002), p.46.

17. John Calvin, ed. John T. McNeill, translated by Ford Lewis Battles, *Institutes of the Christian Religion*, Library of

Christian Classics, Volume 20 (London: SCM Press, 1959), I:1:1 and 2, pp.35–37.

18. Heschel, *Who is Man?*, p.111.

19. From the song, 'Could it be?' on the album *Present Reality* (The Sparrow Corporation, 1988).

20. Peter Kreeft, *Three Philosophies of Life* (San Francisco: St Ignatius Press, 1989), p.93.

21. Jeffrey H. Boyd, 'Self Concept: In Defence of the Word Soul', in Mark McMinn and Timothy R. Phillips (eds.), *Care for the Soul* (Downers Grove: IVP, 2001), pp.102–117. The citation from Rieff is on p.106.

22. Dietrich Bonhoeffer, *Letters and Papers from Prison* (London: Collins, 1968), p.115.

23. Cited by Os Guinness, *The Call* (Nashville: Word, 1998), p.94.

24. Paul Tournier, *The Meaning of Persons* (London: SCM Press, 1957), p.171.

25. Jürgen Moltmann, 'The Pit – Where was God? Jewish and Christian Theology after Auschwitz', in his *God for a Secular Society: The Public Relevance of Theology* (London: SCM Press, 1999), p.173.

26. T.S. Eliot, 'Choruses from "The Rock"', in *Selected Poems* (London: Faber & Faber, 1948), p.117.

Q1

1. Gerhard von Rad, *Genesis* (London: SCM, 1972), p.91.

2. Cited by Ray S. Anderson, *Self Care: A Theology of Personal Empowerment and Spiritual Healing*

(Wheaton: Bridgepoint/Victor, 1995), pp.146ff. This whole
section draws heavily on Anderson's discussion.

3. Christopher Lasch, *The Revolt of the Elites and the Betrayal of Democracy* (New York: W.W. Norton, 1995), pp.222, 198.

4. Anderson, *Self Care* pp.144ff.

5. Cited by David A. de Silva, *Honor, Patronage, Kinship and Purity: Unlocking New Testament Culture* (Downers Grove: IVP, 2000), p.89.

6. Ibid., p.91.

7. Ibid., p.92.

8. Smedes, *Shame and Grace*, p.17.

9. Ibid., pp.40–41.

10. Ibid., pp.17–27.

11. Ibid., p.40.

12. Jimmy Long, *Generating Hope* (London: Marshall Pickering, 1999), pp.101–118.

13. De Silva, *Honor, Patronage, Kinship and Purity*, p.92.

14. Karl Barth, *Evangelical Theology* (Edinburgh: T. & T. Clark, 1963), pp.83–84.

15. R.C. Sproul, *If there is a God why are there Atheists?* (Minneapolis: Bethany Press, 1978), p.69.

16. F.B. Meyer, *Great Men of the Bible* (Grand Rapids: Zondervan 1982 edition), pp.93–94, 91.

17. C.S. Lewis, *Surprised by Joy* (London: Fontana, 1959), pp.181–182.

18. Dietrich Bonhoeffer, *Creation and Fall, and Temptation* (New York: Simon & Schuster, 1997), p.81.

19. Sproul, *If there is a God why are there Atheists?*, p.126.
20. Tom Smail, *Windows on the Cross* (London: Darton, Longman & Todd, 1995), p.10.
21. Miroslav Volf, *Exclusion and Embrace: A Theological Exploration of Identity, Otherness, and Reconciliation* (Nashville: Abingdon Press, 1996), p.126.
22. Corrie ten Boom with John and Elizabeth Sherill, *The Hiding Place* (London: Hodder, 1971), p.182.
23. Richard John Neuhaus, *Death on a Friday Afternoon: Meditations on the Last Words of Jesus from the Cross* (New York: Basic Books, 2000), p.35.
24. Ten Boom, *The Hiding Place*, p.202.
25. Joseph Hart, 'Come ye sinners, poor and wretched', *Methodist Hymn Book*, 324.

Q2

1. William Willimon, *Shaped by the Bible* (Nashville: Abingdon Press, 1990), p.81.
2. Flannery O'Connor, in Sally Fitzgerald (ed.), *The Habit of Being* (New York: Random House, 1979), p.477.
3. Bonhoeffer, *Creation and Fall*, p.72.
4. Derek Kidner, *Genesis* (London: Tyndale Press, 1967), pp.68–69.
5. Jonathan Glover, *Humanity: The Moral History of the Twentieth Century* (London: Pimlico, 2001), pp.280–281. This brilliant book is a searing indictment of godless idealism and its disastrous consequences. It is grim but vastly enlightening.

6. Abraham Heschel, *I Asked for Wonder* (New York: Crossroad, 1986), p.96.

7. Cited in Elizabeth Achtemeier, *Nature, God and Pulpit* (Grand Rapids: Eerdmans, 1992), p.38.

8. Glover, *Humanity*, p.305.

9. For this testimony by Havel and the citation from Solzhenitsyn see Os Guinness, *Time for Truth* (Leicester: IVP), pp.10–11.

10. This comment of Ms Toynbee's is from a news source I can no longer trace.

11. Cited by David Ford, *The Shape of Living* (Grand Rapids: Baker Books, 1997), pp.30–31.

12. Walter Brueggemann, *Interpretation and Obedience* (Minneapolis: Fortress Press, 1991), p.14.

13. Stanley Hauerwas, *Sanctify Them in the Truth* (Edinburgh: T. & T. Clark, 1998), pp.197–198.

14. Roberta Bondi, *Memories of God* (London: Darton, Longman & Todd, 1995), p.25, and for the citations that follow, pp.27, 31.

15. Ibid., p.41.

16. Lewis B. Smedes, *How Can It Be Alright When Everything Is All Wrong?* (San Francisco: Harper, 1982, 1992), p.140.

17. F.W. Faber, in the hymn 'O come and mourn with me awhile'.

Q3

1. Lewis B. Smedes, *A Pretty Good Person* (San Francisco: Harper & Row, 1990), pp.57–71.
2. Ravi Zacharias, *Cries from the Heart* (Nashville: Word, 1998), p.93.
3. Os Guinness, *The Call* (Nashville: Word, 1998), p.91.
4. Dan Allender and Tremper Longman III, *The Cry of the Soul: How Our Emotions Reveal Our Deepest Questions about God* (Christchurch: Nav Press, 1994), p.199.
5. Ted Peters, *Sin: Radical Evil in Soul and Society* (Grand Rapids: Eerdmans), p.12.
6. Neuhaus, *Death on a Friday Afternoon*, pp.15–20. I am indebted to Father Neuhaus's discussion throughout this section.
7. Kidner, *Genesis*, p.68.
8. John Donne (1572–1631), in *The Lion Christian Poetry Collection* compiled by Mary Batchelor (Oxford: Lion, 1995). Poems by Donne, George Herbert and Henry Vaughan – the seventeenth-century metaphysical poets – have been set to music and sung on a wonderful album by Garth Hewitt and Penelope Cave (Chain of Love Music/Sea Dream Music: Eagle, 1992. CD EAG002).
9. Neuhaus, *Death on a Friday Afternoon*, p.34.
10. John 18:35, as noted by my friend Bruce Milne in his fine exposition of John's Gospel, *The Message of John*, The Bible Speaks Today (Leicester: IVP, 1993), p.278.
11. Smail, *Windows on the Cross*, p.50.

Q4

1. Cornelius Plantinga, *Not the Way It's Supposed to Be: A Breviary of Sin* (Grand Rapids: Eerdmans, 1995), p.165.

2. Allender and Longman III, *The Cry of the Soul*, p.58.

3. C.S. Lewis, *Letters to Malcolm: Chiefly on Prayer* (London: Geoffrey Bles,1964), p.126.

4. Christopher Lasch, *The Revolt of the Elites and Betrayal of Democracy* (New York: W.W. Norton, 1995), p.244.

5. Frederick Buechner, *Wishful Thinking* (London: Mowbray, 1993), p.2.

6. Anderson, *Self Care*, p.74. This section owes much to Anderson's insightful discussion.

7. Ibid., p.90.

8. Abel's name may derive from the word *hebel*, 'vanity' or 'nothingness' (cf. Eccl. 1:2). See Willem A. van Gemeren, *New International Dictionary of Old Testament Theology and Exegesis*, vol. 4 (Carlisle: Paternoster Press, 1997), p.361; Claus Westermann, *Genesis 1-11* (London: SPCK, 1984), p.292; Gordon J. Wenham, *Genesis 1-15* (Waco: Word, 1987), p.102.

9. Peter de Vries, *The Blood of the Lamb* (Middlesex: Penguin Books, 1969), p.169.

10. Anderson, *Self Care*, p.74.

11. Plantinga, *Not the Way It's Supposed to Be*, p.181.

12. Elizabeth Achtemeier, *Minor Prophets 1*, New International Biblical Commentary (Peabody: Hendrickson, 1996), pp.283-284.

13. Most famously in C.S. Lewis's sermon, 'The Weight of

Glory', in *They Asked for a Paper: Papers and Addresses* (London: Geoffrey Bles, 1962), pp.197–211.

14. Sam Storms, *Pleasures Evermore* (Colorado: Nav Press, 2000), p.27.

15. Ibid., p.33.

16. Anderson, *Self Care* p.47.

17. Rebecca Manley Pippert, *A Heart Like His* (London: IVP, 1996), p.178.

18. Henri Nouwen, *The Return of the Prodigal Son* (London: Darton, Longman & Todd, 1992), p.98. Nouwen's wonderful reflections on the parable as depicted in Rembrandt's famous painting now in the Hermitage are, as I can testify, especially effective in shaping a life-changing spiritual retreat.

19. De Vries, *The Blood of the Lamb* pp.181–186.

20. Fanny Crosby, in the hymn, 'Rescue the perishing', *Methodist Hymn Book*, 338.

Q5

1. Martin Luther King, ed. Coretta Scott King, *The Words of Martin Luther King* (London: Fount, 1985), p.95.

2. Hugo Gryn with Naomi Gryn, *Chasing Shadows* (London: Viking, 2000), pp.248–251.

3. Douglas John Hall, *Imaging God: Dominion as Stewardship* (Grand Rapids: Eerdmans, 1986), p.128.

4. David Ford, *The Shape of Living*, pp.29ff.

5. Eugene H. Peterson, *The Contemplative Pastor* (Grand Rapids: Eerdmans, 1989), p.126.

6. Christopher de Vinck, *The Power of the Powerless* (London: Hodder & Stoughton, 1989), p.9.

7. Wendell Berry, 'The Conservation of Nature and the Preservation of Humanity', in *Another Turn of the Crank* (Washington: Counterpoint, 1995), p.83.

8. Ibid., p.80.

9. Eliot, 'Choruses from "The Rock"'.

10. The phrase is from the Orthodox theologian Anthony Ugolnik, *The Illuminating Icon* (Grand Rapids: Eerdmans, 1989), p.122. 'In the very persons of the Godhead, "proceeding" in perfect love from their interrelationship, we experience a vortex of love that pulls us as well into its power.'

11. Richard Bauckham and Trevor Hart, *At the Cross: Meditations on People Who Were There* (London: Darton, Longman & Todd, 1999), p.122.

12. Ronald S. Wallace, *Words of Triumph: The Words from the Cross and Their Application Today* (Richmond: John Knox Press, 1964), p.43.

13. Neuhaus, *Death on a Friday Afternoon*, p.94.

14. John V. Taylor, *The Go-Between God: The Holy Spirit and the Christian Mission* (London: SCM Press, 1972), pp.127–128.

15. Victor P. Hamilton, *Genesis 1–17*, NICOT (Grand Rapids: Eerdmans 1990), p.232.

16. William L. Lane, *Hebrews 9–13*, Word Biblical Commentary (Dallas: Word, 1991), p.474.

17. Philip Edgecumbe Hughes, *A Commentary on the Letter*

to the Hebrews (Grand Rapids: Eerdmans, 1977), p.551.

18. Oliver O'Donovan, *Resurrection and Moral Order* (Leicester: IVP, 1986), p.74.

RSVP

1. Plantinga, *Not The Way It's Supposed To Be*, p.197.

POSTSCRIPT

1. W.B.Yeats, 'The Second Coming'.
2. John Oman, *Grace and Personality* (London: Fontana, 1917, 1962), pp.111, 176.
3. Mark Buchanan, *Your God is Too Safe* (Oregon: Multnomah, 2001), p.97.
4. G.K. Chesterton, *Orthodoxy* (London: The Bodley Head, 1927), p.297.
5. Karl Rahner, *The Eternal Year* (London: Burns & Oates, 1964), pp.55–56.
6. Ten Boom, *The Hiding Place*, p.182.

NATIONAL DISTRIBUTORS

UK: (and countries not listed below)
CWR, Waverley Abbey House, Waverley Lane, Farnham, Surrey GU9 8EP.
Tel: (01252) 784710 Outside UK (44) 1252 784710

AUSTRALIA: CMC Australasia, PO Box 519, Belmont, Victoria 3216.
Tel: (03) 5241 3288

CANADA: Cook Communications Ministries, PO Box 98, 55 Woodslee Avenue,
Paris, Ontario.
Tel: 1800 263 2664

GHANA: Challenge Enterprises of Ghana, PO Box 5723, Accra.
Tel: (021) 222437/223249 Fax: (021) 226227

HONG KONG: Cross Communications Ltd, 1/F, 562A Nathan Road, Kowloon.
Tel: 2780 1188 Fax: 2770 6229

INDIA: Crystal Communications, 10-3-18/4/1, East Marredpally, Secunderabad – 500 026.
Tel/Fax: (040) 7732801

KENYA: Keswick Books and Gifts Ltd, PO Box 10242, Nairobi.
Tel: (02) 331692/226047 Fax: (02) 728557

MALAYSIA: Salvation Book Centre (M) Sdn Bhd, 23 Jalan SS 2/64,
47300 Petaling Jaya, Selangor.
Tel: (03) 78766411/78766797 Fax: (03) 78757066/78756360

NEW ZEALAND: CMC Australasia, PO Box 36015, Lower Hutt.
Tel: 0800 449 408 Fax: 0800 449 049

NIGERIA: FBFM, Helen Baugh House, 96 St Finbarr's College Road, Akoka, Lagos.
Tel: (01) 7747429/4700218/825775/827264

PHILIPPINES: OMF Literature Inc, 776 Boni Avenue, Mandaluyong City.
Tel: (02) 531 2183 Fax: (02) 531 1960

REPUBLIC OF IRELAND: Scripture Union, 40 Talbot Street, Dublin 1.
Tel: (01) 8363764

SINGAPORE: Armour Publishing Pte Ltd, Block 203A Henderson Road,
11-06 Henderson Industrial Park, Singapore 159546.
Tel: 6 276 9976 Fax: 6 276 7564

SOUTH AFRICA: Struik Christian Books, 80 MacKenzie Street, PO Box 1144,
Cape Town 8000.
Tel: (021) 462 4360 Fax: (021) 461 3612

SRI LANKA: Christombu Books, 27 Hospital Street, Colombo 1.
Tel: (01) 433142/328909

TANZANIA: CLC Christian Book Centre, PO Box 1384, Mkwepu Street, Dar es Salaam.
Tel/Fax (022) 2119439

USA: Cook Communications Ministries, PO Box 98, 55 Woodslee Avenue, Paris,
Ontario, Canada.
Tel: 1800 263 2664

ZIMBABWE: Word of Life Books, Shop 4, Memorial Building, 35 S Machel Avenue, Harare.
Tel: (04) 781305 Fax: (04) 774739

For email addresses, visit the CWR website: www.cwr.org.uk

CWR is a registered charity – number 294387

Trusted
All Over the World

Daily Devotionals

Books and Videos

Day and Residential Courses

Counselling Training

Biblical Study Courses

Regional Seminars

Ministry to Women

CWR have been providing training and resources for Christians since the 1960s. From our headquarters at Waverley Abbey House we have been serving God's people with a vision to help apply God's Word to everyday life and relationships. The daily devotional *Every Day with Jesus* is read by over three-quarters of a million people in more than 150 countries, and our unique courses in biblical studies and pastoral care are respected all over the world.

For a free brochure about our seminars and courses or a catalogue of CWR resources please contact us at the following address:

CWR,
Waverley Abbey House,
Waverley Lane,
Farnham,
Surrey GU9 8EP

Telephone: 01252 784700
Email: mail@cwr.org.uk
Website: www.cwr.org.uk

CWR CRUSADE FOR WORLD REVIVAL *Applying God's Word to everyday life and relationships*

Leadership

An inspiring and challenging model for Christian leaders
today. Philip Greenslade draws on his experience in Christian
leadership to outline the characteristics of a true leader,
illustrating the five-fold ministry embodied in Christ.

Using the biblical ideals found in Jesus, Paul and other great
saints in Scripture and history, the writer takes us to the heart
of the kind of leader God is looking for to lead His people.
An essential and inspiring read for anyone in ministry.

'This book is one of my all-time favourites and a classic.
It challenges inadequate views of both the Church and her
leadership. Its treatment of the controversial present-day
work of the five-fold ministry in Ephesians 4 is masterly.'

Greg Haslam
Minister, Westminster Chapel, London

£7.99
ISBN 1-85345-202-5

God's Story

This exciting Bible reading programme takes you on a journey
of discovery through Scripture – promise by promise. Each
major covenant is explored in-depth to reveal a connected
narrative which ultimately leads to Jesus.

- 365 undated daily readings – start at any point in the year
- Selected Bible readings, taking between 10 to 15
  minutes each day
- Experience the Bible as an enthralling narrative
- Visit www.cover2cover.org for Bible features and
  discussion forum

£9.95
ISBN 1-85345-186-X